THE CONSTRUCTION OF THE SUPERNATURAL IN EURO-AMERICAN CULTURES

SCIENTIFIC STUDIES OF RELIGION: INQUIRY AND EXPLANATION

Series editors: Luther H. Martin, Donald Wiebe, Radek Kundt and Dimitris Xygalatas

Scientific Studies of Religion: Inquiry and Explanation publishes cutting-edge research in the new and growing field of scientific studies in religion. Its aim is to publish empirical, experimental, historical, and ethnographic research on religious thought, behaviour, and institutional structures. The series works with a broad notion of scientific that includes innovative work on understanding religion(s), both past and present. With an emphasis on the cognitive science of religion, the series includes complementary approaches to the study of religion, such as psychology and computer modelling of religious data. Titles seek to provide explanatory accounts for the religious behaviors under review, both past and present.

The Attraction of Religion, edited by D. Jason Slone and James A. Van Slyke
The Cognitive Science of Religion, edited by D. Jason Slone and William W. McCorkle Jr.
Contemporary Evolutionary Theories of Culture and the Study of Religion, Radek Kundt
Death Anxiety and Religious Belief, Jonathan Jong and Jamin Halberstadt
Gnosticism and the History of Religions, David G. Robertson
The Impact of Ritual on Child Cognition, Veronika Rybanska
Language, Cognition, and Biblical Exegesis, edited by Ronit Nikolsky, Istvan Czachesz, Frederick S. Tappenden and Tamas Biro
The Learned Practice of Religion in the Modern University, Donald Wiebe
The Mind of Mithraists, Luther H. Martin
Naturalism and Protectionism in the Study of Religion, Juraj Franek
New Patterns for Comparative Religion, William E. Paden
Philosophical Foundations of the Cognitive Science of Religion, Robert N. McCauley with E. Thomas Lawson
Religion Explained?, edited by Luther H. Martin and Donald Wiebe
Religion in Science Fiction, Steven Hrotic
Religious Evolution and the Axial Age, Stephen K. Sanderson
The Roman Mithras Cult, Olympia Panagiotidou with Roger Beck
Solving the Evolutionary Puzzle of Human Cooperation, Glenn Barenthin
Understanding Religion through Artificial Intelligence, Justin E. Lane

THE CONSTRUCTION OF THE SUPERNATURAL IN EURO-AMERICAN CULTURES

Something Nice about Vampires

BENSON SALER

BLOOMSBURY ACADEMIC
LONDON · NEW YORK · OXFORD · NEW DELHI · SYDNEY

BLOOMSBURY ACADEMIC
Bloomsbury Publishing Plc
50 Bedford Square, London, WC1B 3DP, UK
1385 Broadway, New York, NY 10018, USA
29 Earlsfort Terrace, Dublin 2, Ireland

BLOOMSBURY, BLOOMSBURY ACADEMIC and the Diana logo
are trademarks of Bloomsbury Publishing Plc

First published in Great Britain 2022
This paperback edition published 2023

Copyright © Benson Saler, 2022

Benson Saler has asserted his right under the Copyright, Designs
and Patents Act, 1988, to be identified as Author of this work.

For legal purposes the Acknowledgments on p. xxiii constitute
an extension of this copyright page.

All rights reserved. No part of this publication may be reproduced or
transmitted in any form or by any means, electronic or mechanical, including
photocopying, recording, or any information storage or retrieval system,
without prior permission in writing from the publishers.

Bloomsbury Publishing Plc does not have any control over, or responsibility for,
any third-party websites referred to or in this book. All internet addresses given
in this book were correct at the time of going to press. The author and publisher
regret any inconvenience caused if addresses have changed or sites have
ceased to exist, but can accept no responsibility for any such changes.

A catalogue record for this book is available from the British Library.

A catalog record for this book is available from the Library of Congress.
Library of Congress Control Number: 2021945704

ISBN:	HB:	978-1-3502-3949-4
	PB:	978-1-3502-3953-1
	ePDF:	978-1-3502-3950-0
	eBook:	978-1-3502-3951-7

Series: Scientific Studies of Religion: Inquiry and Explanation

Typeset by Integra Software Services Pvt. Ltd.

To find out more about our authors and books visit www.bloomsbury.com
and sign up for our newsletters

In memory of David Flusser and Shlomo Pines

"Supernatural agency is the most culturally recurrent, cognitively relevant, and evolutionarily compelling concept in religion. The concept of the supernatural is culturally derived from an innate cognitive schema." (Scott Atran 1990)

"The supernatural comes in two varieties: more or less serious. Serious scholars often ignore the nonserious stuff, and they are wrong to do so." (Pascal Boyer 2001: 89)

CONTENTS

Benson Saler—An Appreciation viii
Preface xxii
Acknowledgments xxiii

Introduction 1

1 Social Scientists and the Supernatural 15

2 Nature and Transcendence among the Ancient Greeks 37

3 Some Theological Perspectives 67

4 Something Nice about Vampires 101

5 Dracula and Carmilla: Monsters and the Mind 105

6 Toward a Realistic and Relevant "Science of Religion" 117

Notes 150
Bibliography 152
Index 159

BENSON SALER—AN APPRECIATION

Benson Saler passed away in his sleep on February 25, 2021, a few months before his ninety-first birthday. We mourn this passing of a brilliant but humble intellectual, a dedicated anthropologist, and a kind and humorous person. It is an honor for me to write this appreciation.

Benson was first and foremost a cultural anthropologist, with an early interest in human psychology, and, since the 1990s, he was an active figure in the growing cognitive science of religion. He was also an astute philosopher, often drawing attention to what he called the "facile assumptions" of his fellow anthropologists and showing them where they were wrong about a number of central concepts. As the title of the last chapter in this volume indicates, Benson also worked toward developing "a realistic and relevant science of religion."

Along the way, however, he has treated us to his dry sense of humor. The collection of chapters in this volume has a few priceless examples of his humor. Here are two: "Many readers of these lines can probably describe a unicorn more easily and (with respect to widespread Euro-American conventions) more accurately than they can describe an aardvark" (p. 6). In the last chapter of this volume, Benson introduces himself in the following manner: "In approaching the country that some call 'the science of religion,' I feel obliged to identify myself as a sympathetic alien. In light of certain of my research interests, moreover, I hasten to add that I am fully terrestrial. But my passport is from an anthropology department rather than from a department of religion" (p. 117).

His research and publications fall into the following categories (with due respect to Benson's skepticism of "categories"): Native American Indians in Guatemala and South America, currents and cults in contemporary

United States, the history of ideas in anthropology and the study of religion, categorizations in the study of religion, and the cognitive science of religion.

Already in his work with the Quiché Maya during the late 1950s, Benson showed an interest in the quirky sides of life. He had a knack of using his ethnographic data and interviews in concert with his deep knowledge of the literature to raise important issues that in one way or another questioned or challenged generally accepted views held by the big names in ethnography and anthropology. A good example is his work on various religious specialists among the Quiché Maya in the pueblo of Santiago El Palmar. In his article on nagual, witch, and sorcerer (Saler 1964), he deftly pulls out the rug from under the assumed truths of scholarship on "nagualism" in Middle America and provides an in-depth analysis of the term "nagual" as understood by his informants. Here we see that it can be used to describe an affinity between some people and a living animal but is also the word describing the zodiac, the day in the Quiché Maya calendar that a person is born on, the Catholic patron saint of El Palmar, and an Indian medium claimed to be suffering from possession by the Earth Essence, El Mundo. The article contains a very enlightening discussion of transforming witches and sorcerers.

A quirky experience in his fieldwork was described in a 1962 article published, appropriately, in the *Psychoanalysis and Psychoanalytic Review* entitled "Unsuccessful Practitioners in a Bicultural Guatemalan Community" (Saler 1962). The above-mentioned Indian medium, whom Benson calls Aj-nawal Mesa ("One who pertains to the Spiritual Essence of the Table"), uncharacteristically took on the aspects of the local Ladino spiritualists and performed possession states under the influence of El Mundo. As his initial success grew, he started manipulating and swindling his clients, making ludicrous pronouncements and demanding outrageous prices for his sessions. Eventually he lost his clients and his business. Benson described a séance in the village of El Palmar conducted for his wife Joyce (who was posing as a client) by an Indian spiritualist. The latter wanting to humiliate Benson for some reason, hysterically cried out during the séance that he could not heal Joyce's alleged toothache because her husband was a shaman. The reaction in the pueblo was disgust with the medium. Everyone knew that Benson, being an outsider, was not a shaman, so the medium, they said, was a liar.[1]

He describes other curious matters, such as the departure of a troublesome volcano god in the area, who decided to move to Mexico instead where business was better. Benson's interest in strange ideas and cults continued with his coauthored book on UFO cultists in the United States and his study of vampires in this volume (see especially the chapter provocatively titled "Something Nice about Vampires"). His work on UFO cultists (*UFO Crash at Roswell: The Genesis of a Modern Myth*, 1997) came as a surprise for some of us, but as he and his coauthors note in the introduction: "the Roswell Incident is a significant cultural phenomenon and, as such, can be analyzed using the theoretical tools and concepts of cultural anthropology" (Saler, Ziegler, and Moore 1997:xi). And, indeed, they also note that understanding this phenomenon will tell us more "about ourselves and about the society in which we live" (p. xii) than about extraterrestrial beings. The book was coauthored with Charles A. Ziegler (an anthropologist colleague at Brandeis with whom Benson has cowritten a number of publications) and Charles B. Moore (professor emeritus of atmospheric physics at the New Mexico Institute of Mining and Technology). Moore was project engineer of the Constant Level Balloon Group from New York University who in 1947 launched in Alamorgordo, New Mexico, three balloon trains capable of floating between 10 and 20 kilometers for forty-eight hours. The balloon trains were developed to detect high-altitude sound waves (p. 4). One of the trains was hit by a summer monsoon and the wreckage fell down on the ranchlands of William W. Brazel, some 120 kilometers from Roswell. This wreckage became the first source of the Roswell myth. The book consists of technical details by Moore about this incident as well as an analysis by Ziegler of how and by whom the Roswell myth developed. Benson's chapter explores the interesting idea that elements of the myth resemble elements associated with religion. In order to proceed along these lines, Benson discusses the issue of the definition of religion. In drawing on his early ideas about definition in terms of family resemblances (see below), Benson argued that the UFO movement has religious elements in that there are alien superhumans, a metaphysical-cosmological dualism, an eschatology, rituals and sacralized social activities, and stimulation of powerful emotions (p. 148).

Benson's interest in vampires has a different slant. In this collection of chapters, Ziegler and Benson present their comparative analysis of Bram Stoker's *Dracula* of 1897 and Le Fanu's *Carmilla* of 1872. Why, they ask, is Dracula more famous and more influential in Western culture than Carmilla, which has greater literary distinction? They refer to prototype theory, but more importantly, they draw on cognitive and evolutionary theories. They argue that Dracula fits more closely our evolved architecture of mind. The power of the narrative lies in the monstrous aspects of Dracula and the existence of a monster-slayer. The monstrous aspects, they claim, stem from our evolutionary experience as both predators and prey. Selection occurred for "neurologically grounded dispositions to apperceive, and to respond to, predatory threats" (this volume, p. 111). With reference to Pascal Boyer's work, the monster/monster-slayer theme, which is widespread throughout human history, contains all of the salience and relevance in our heritage by stimulating mental systems of fear and predation avoidance. These ideas are "cognitively optimal," as Boyer argues, and thus are remembered and transmitted. Vampires have just the right number of counterintuitive elements.

Benson made his mark in method and theory in the study of religion in two ways—first and foremost, his skepticism and problematization of categories and concepts. Categorization is both the bane and bones of academic scholarship, but Benson delved into the history of concepts, such as "religion" or the "supernatural," and not only asked fellow scholars to be aware of the pitfalls of categorization but also tried to solve some of the problems that concepts and categories cause. Here we see his use of prototype theory especially in his definitive book on the concept of religion (Saler 1993). Secondly, Benson has consistently voiced his frustration with fellow anthropologists on a variety of matters and shown how cognitive and evolutionary approaches can resolve some of those frustrations. And in this context, he draws inspiration mostly from the work of Pascal Boyer.

As mentioned, Benson worried a lot about concepts. Not only concepts like "religion" and the "supernatural," but also concepts like the "natural," "similarity," "belief," "intuition," "nagualism," "vampires," "ethnocentrism," "essentialism," "nominalism," "universals," "interpretation," and so on are carefully but tenaciously deconstructed. In his learned contribution to my Festschrift, Benson even deconstructs deconstructionism and the whole idea of "cause" and "effect." Although contemporary physicists are raising the possibility of phenomena in the universe for which there are no causes, he notes: "But if physicists begin to talk like theologians, some of us are likely to become nervous. Were we, moreover, to compare some contemporary physicists to deconstructionists, the deconstructionists might suddenly strike us as being good-old-boys rather than radicals or nihilists, for they, too, cede place to causality, their novel experiments and pronouncements on language notwithstanding" (Saler 2019:278).

Through careful and faithful, however critical, discussions of various scholars in the history of a particular idea or concept, Benson has struggled with concepts such as the supernatural,[2] beliefs,[3] and religion[4] for decades. I cannot determine when he began formulating his prototype theory of religion, but it was well before his signal work *Conceptualizing Religion: Immanent Anthropologists, Transcendent Natives, and Unbounded Categories* of 1993. He certainly was acquainted with family resemblance theory as indicated in his 1974 review of Rodney Needham's book *Belief, Language, and Experience* (Saler 1974). Perhaps his paper presented at the 1990 World Congress of the International Association for the History of Religions in Rome entitled

"Cultural Anthropology and the Definition of Religion"[5] was the earliest sketch of his solution to the problem. In acknowledging the complexity of the phenomenon in that paper, Benson called for a multi-factorial approach inspired by Ludwig Wittgenstein's "family resemblances" and biologists' "polythetic classification." In his discussion of games, Wittgenstein argued that the variety of what we call games do not share a single quality or feature. Rather, they share more or less similarities. The same can be said of those cultural phenomena that we call "religion" (Saler 1993:832). Benson points out that the use of "polythetic classification" is highly problematical for the social sciences and, instead, he turns to the prototype theory of cognitive scientists, such as Eleanor Rosch. He quotes Rosch: "By prototypes of categories, we have generally meant the clearest cases of category membership defined operationally by people's judgments of goodness of membership in the category" (Rosch 1978:36; Saler 1994:835).

In his book *Conceptualizing Religion*, Benson fully develops his application of the two above-mentioned approaches. In a very learned, eloquent, and wide-ranging history of approaches to the definition of religion, ranging from anthropologists, historians, and philosophers to theologians and scholars of religion, Benson suggests, in his critique of monothetic definitions, that it would be better to approach universals "as a matter of costs and benefits rather than ontology" (p. 155) and argues:

> But do the benefits of talking about universals as if they have an objective or independent existence outweigh the costs (calculated in terms of metaphysical baggage)? Perhaps in linguistics and in some other fields the costs are slight or otherwise justifiable. For students of religion (kinship, law, etc.), however, the costs, in my opinion, are a needless extravagance. That is because everything worthwhile that scholars might hope to gain in such cases by affirming universals can be accomplished by positing resemblances. (p. 156)

This is exactly what he does at the end of the book: "My suggestion for conceptualizing religion is this: Religion is an abstraction. For analytical purposes we may conceptualize it in terms of a pool of elements that more or less tend to occur together in the best exemplars of the category" (p. 225). He is thinking of Judaisms, Christianities, and Islams as prototypical and suggests that we formally acknowledge what "many of us do informally" (p. 212). He readily admits that it does not resolve the problem of identifying religions other than Western monotheisms (p. 226), but each case must be cogently analyzed. "We decide," Benson writes, "by reasoned arguments the question of whether or not to include under the rubric religion candidates that strike us as representing lesser degrees of prototypicality." But, he continues, "we do so in the absence of certitude about, and firm commitments to, boundaries" (p. 225). Is this ethnocentric? Yes, he answers, "but how could it be otherwise?" (p. 261):

> Now, I confess to being "ethnocentric" in a certain sense, but I contend that I am productively rather than outrageously so. And I do not privilege the Western monotheisms because I personally deem them superior to other religions, or the most evolved forms of religiosity, or anything of the sort. Rather, those families of religion are connected in complex ways to the development of religion as a Western category, and ideas about them continue to influence how Westerners and persons educated in the West use the term religion. Because of that, the Western monotheisms might be used—if critical monitoring is employed—as markers that map a productive starting place. (p. 227)

He does suggest, however, that we should seriously consider using selected native categories and "experiment with them as transcultural tools" (p. 263).

Such a clear standpoint invites challenge. And such was the case in which Benson's book was the subject of a review symposium in the journal *Method and Theory in the Study of Religion*, which I coedited together with Russell T. McCutcheon and Scott S. Elliott, as a special issue consisting of papers presented at the XVIIth World Congress of the International Association for the History of Religions in Mexico City, 1995 (Geertz, McCutcheon, and Elliott 2000). The symposium consisted of papers by Gary Lease, Russell T. McCutcheon, William E. Paden, and Don Wiebe, followed by Benson's response. Although they all welcomed Benson's contribution to theoretical analysis, they also rejected or problematized some of his central ideas: Lease argued that we on the contrary need boundaries in our definitions; McCutcheon disagreed with Benson's stance on ethnocentrism and specifically on using native categories; Paden raised issues about the limitations of prototype theory; and Wiebe raised issues on the limitations of family resemblance theory. All of them, however, recognized Benson's deep understanding of conceptualization issues and their history. One thing is for sure: he had formulated reasons for every concept he uses.

Benson's foraging into cognitive science is in some ways connected with his dissatisfaction with fellow anthropologists. In this volume, he notes "an unfortunate proclivity traditionally evinced by many of my fellow anthropologists: the investiture of culture with powers and importance that go beyond compelling attributions." It must be said in the same breath, however: "But, as sometimes happens in corrective movements, the pendulum occasionally swings too far in the other direction, and some proponents of the cognitive science of religion, in my opinion, do not always accord culture the attention and significance that it deserves." I agree with him on both counts. Benson does not agree with the popular bias that culture "molds" the behavior of people, nor that anthropology is the "Study of Culture." It is rather the "Study of Human Beings," as implied in the term itself. And in this sense, scholars must not abandon explanatory theory in the study of religion. The cognitive and evolutionary sciences of religion, Benson says, "strike me as being generally more intrigued by the explanatory possibilities of innateness than were their predecessors and some of their present-day successors" (this volume, p. 104).

This emphasis on human nature is crucial to understanding Benson's interest in the cognitive sciences. As noted above in his characterization of what should be our purpose in studying UFO cults, and as he formulated in his Conceptualization book: "if our ultimate purpose as scholars is to say interesting things about human beings rather than about religions and religion, appreciation of the pervasiveness of religious elements in human life is far more important than any contrivance for bounding religion" (Saler 1993:226). More to the point, concerning the cognitive science of religion (CSR), he writes that it is commendable because "its conceptual reach neither begins nor ends with religion. It seeks to explain religion by considering human beings in existential and evolutionary perspectives, it treats religion as a fuzzy set of various expressions of our emergent humanity, and it ends … with interesting postulations about what it means to be human" (Saler 2010:331).

Benson's interest in cognition has long been much broader than CSR's primary focus on mental representations, evidenced for instance in his coauthored 1966 commentary on a paper by anthropologist George Foster concerning a hypothesized "cognitive orientation" among Tzintzuntzan peasants in the Mexican State of Michoacán (Kaplan and Saler 1966). Their criticism mostly concerns Foster's opaque selection method in using field data to determine the communal cognitive orientation model that he hypothesized. They also criticize him for being unclear about causality between cognitive orientation, social patterns, and behavior. Furthermore, they point out that there is disagreement among componential analysts about moving from "structural reality" to "psychological reality" (pp. 204–5). Thus, Benson demonstrated very early on his knowledge about cognitive approaches in the social sciences and his concerns about causality in the cognitive sciences.

Perhaps the best entrance into Benson's opinions about the CSR is his 2010 article "Theory and Criticism: The Cognitive Science of Religion" (Saler 2010).

He begins with the cogent observation: "I do not think that proponents of CSR have connected up all of the dots in their efforts to explain religion. Indeed, I do not think that they have identified all of the dots. But I do think that they are the most exciting game in town" (p. 331). As a point of departure, however, he characterizes how CSR answers the question of why people are religious. He notes that CSR folks claim that humans have religion "because evolution has endowed them with a certain kind of mind" (p. 333) and, therefore, the best procedure is to generate "reliable information about the nature and development of the human mind" (p. 333). They draw consequently on scientific methodologies that place "a premium on the systematic and replicable testing or evaluating of claims to knowledge" (p. 333).

He identifies three aspects that attract him. First, CSR "takes human beings rather than religions and cultures as its phenomenal subjects" (p. 334). Second, the cognitive processes that CSR proponents maintain "are much the same as those that enable and support other aspects of human life" (p. 334). Third, CSR is "for the most part realistically and moderately reductive in its explanatory efforts, in keeping with what is usually the case in the sciences" (p. 334). The main criticism brought against CSR theorizing by critics is exemplified by Barbara Herrnstein Smith. She argues that the "New Naturalist" program is too simplistic and intellectually confining to explain such a richly complex phenomenon as religion (pp. 335–6; Smith 2009). Although Benson partially agrees with her, he replies that CSR "boldly suggest[s] important consequences of conjectured but plausible inference systems and other cognitive mechanisms claimed to have been established in the course of human evolution. That it does not explain more may be a matter for regret, but one can nevertheless admire it for what it does attempt to explain" (p. 337).

A way forward for CSR, Benson suggests, is to rethink the matter of explanation. Benson unfortunately lumps the Aarhus School (that I co-founded with Jeppe Sinding Jensen) together with Herrnstein Smith. But the point is that "monochromatic explanations of polychromatic phenomena" should be replaced by "polychromatic theorizing"; in other words, "we can and should allow for multi-level and multi-faceted explanations of complex phenomena" (p. 338). Benson recommends that we develop an analogy to epigenetic theorizing in the biological sciences. Thus, similar to geneticists' realization that extra-genetic factors can turn genes on or off, so too can cultural traditions have the same effects on cognitive mechanisms. Despite its narrowness, Benson considers the standard cognitive science of religion model to be "a brilliant achievement" in that "it has 'naturalized' religion more matter-of-factly and more persuasively than any other theory of which I have knowledge. In arguing that religion originated as byproducts of evolutionary developments, Boyer and his cohort align and ally their understandings of religion with what is surely the most successful and powerful of all theories respecting the emergence and fundamental nature of humankind" (p. 338). These are strong words, and I know personally of a number of colleagues in the study of religion who would adamantly, stubbornly, and—dare I say it—prejudicially reject such a claim. My response is, "Right on, Benson, and thanks for the encouragement!"

This brings me to my final point in my appreciation of Benson Saler. I am talking about his ultimate goal of promoting a scientific study of religion. The final chapter in this volume, "Toward a Realistic and Relevant 'Science of Religion,'" is a revised version of a lecture presented in Finland in 2000. It was published in *Method and Theory in the Study of Religion* (Saler 2004) and reprinted in his essay collection *Understanding Religion: Selected Essays* (Saler 2009). I will be referencing the chapter in this volume. In his dissatisfaction with the relevance and realism of many publications by members of both disciplines, Benson proceeds to explicate what he means by "relevant" and "realistic." I will refrain from providing the details of his argument and cut right to the chase. What he means by a relevant and realistic science of religion, which is the ultimate goal of his own work and thought, is this: (1) *relevance* in terms of connecting "their findings and theorizing to the findings and theorizing of other sciences, particularly the biological [i.e., evolutionary] and cognitive sciences" (p. 121), and (2) *realism* in terms of "having to do with accommodations to facts and to good arguments and a corresponding disinclination to accept the fanciful and the illogical" (p. 135). The latter point, I imagine, needs a few more words. By realistic, Benson once again refers to his favorite line of inquiry, namely conceptualization. Following Karl Popper, Benson argues that our concepts must be explicated in order to provide "serviceable clarity" (p. 136). A realistic science of religion, he claims, "requires a realistic explication of 'religion'" (p. 137). After a discussion of his prototype theory of "religion," and a discussion of Pascal Boyer's and Harvey Whitehouse's theories, Benson explains: "Grounded in informed accommodations to the realities of language and categorization rather than in quixotic requirements for transparency and precision, and with relevance to the cognitive and evolutionary sciences, it encourages us both to explore religion and to transcend it" (p. 149). What he means exactly by "transcending religion" is formulated immediately following that sentence: religion is "neither *sui generis* nor autonomous, and so not immune to reductive explanation" (p. 149).

It is appropriate, I think, to quote Benson one last time, as a kind of epithet of his crowning achievements. In his both sympathetic and skeptical analysis of postmodern turns in anthropology, he writes, "We would all be better anthropologists, and better students of religion, I imagine, if we were as self-critical as we sometimes advise ourselves to be" (Saler 1993:150).

Alas, a great man and gentleman scholar has passed away. We will never forget Benson's work or his warm personality. A memorable festive lunch that a group of colleagues and I enjoyed, hosted by Benson and his gracious wife Joyce some ten years ago, left an indelible impression on all of us. After an excellent lunch and spirited conversation, he took us into the living room, where two enormous speakers stood conspicuously in the room. Benson was clearly excited and in a fun mood. Then he put on "These Bones" by the Fairfield Four, and the deep, base song—magnified hugely by the speakers—about the creation of Eve and the fall of mankind washed over us. The ride back to town, to say the least, was meditative.

Benson Saler, we will miss you!

Armin W. Geertz

Religion, Cognition and Culture Research Unit

Department of the Study of Religion

Aarhus, Aarhus University

March 31, 2021

Notes

1 I am grateful to Joyce Saler for background information on this event.

2 He avoids the term in his early papers such as Saler 1962 and 1964, preferring the term "superhuman" or "other-than-human" beings and specifically addresses the issue in his 1977 paper.

3 See Saler 1971, 1972, 1974; Vogt 1972.

4 See his response to Stewart Guthrie's signal article "A Cognitive Theory of Religion" (Guthrie 1980:197), and his paper read at the 1986 Annual Meeting of the American Anthropological Association entitled "*Religio* and the Definition of Religion" (Saler 1987).

5 Published in 1994 in Ugo Bianchi, ed., *The Notion of "Religion" in Comparative Research* (Saler 1994).

Bibliography

Geertz, Armin W., Russell T. McCutcheon, and Scott S. Elliott, editors. 2000. *Perspectives on Method and Theory in the Study of Religion: Adjunct Proceedings of the XVIIth Congress of the International Association for the History of Religions, Mexico City, 1995.* E. J. Brill.

Guthrie, Stewart Elliott. 1980. "A Cognitive Theory of Religion." *Current Anthropology*, vol. 21, no. 2, pp. 181–203.

Kaplan, David, and Benson Saler. 1966. "Foster's 'Image of Limited Good': An Example of Anthropological Explanation." *American Anthropologist*, vol. 68, no. 1, pp. 202–6.

Rosch, Eleanor. 1978. "Principles of Categorization." *Cognition and Categorization*, edited by Eleanor Rosch and B. B. Lloyd, Lawrence Erlbaum, pp. 27–48.

Saler, Benson. 1962. "Unsuccessful Practitioners in a Bicultural Guatemalan Community." *Psychoanalysis and the Psychoanalytic Review*, vol. 49, no. 2, pp. 103–18.

Saler, Benson. 1964. "Nagual, Witch, and Sorcerer in a Quiché Village." *Ethnology*, vol. 3, no. 3, pp. 305–27.

Saler, Benson. 1971. "Review: Zinacantan: *A Maya Community in the Highlands of Chiapas* by Evon Z. Vogt." *American Anthropologist*, vol. 73, no. 2, pp. 338–40.

Saler, Benson. 1972. "A Reply to Vogt." *American Anthropologist*, vol. 74, no. 1–2, p. 202.

Saler, Benson. 1974. "Review: *Belief, Language, and Experience* by Rodney Needham." *American Anthropologist*, vol. 76, no. 4, pp. 861–6.

Saler, Benson. 1977. "Spiritual Power in Santiago El Palmar." *The Anthropology of Power: Ethnographic Studies from Asia, Oceania, and the New World*, edited by Raymond D. Fogelson and Richard N. Adams, Academic Press, pp. 287–97.

Saler, Benson. 1987. "*Religio* and the Definition of Religion." *Cultural Anthropology*, vol. 2, no. 3, pp. 395–9.

Saler, Benson. 1993. *Conceptualizing Religion. Immanent Anthropologists, Transcendent Natives, and Unbounded Categories*. E. J. Brill.

Saler, Benson. 1994. "Cultural Anthropology and the Definition of Religion." *The Notion of "Religion" in Comparative Research. Selected Proceedings of the XVIth Congress of the International Association for the History of Religions, Rome, 3rd–8th September, 1990*, edited by Ugo Bianchi, Fabio Mora and Lorenzo Bianchi, "L'erma" di Bretschneider, pp. 831–6.

Saler, Benson. 2004. "Towards a Realistic and Relevant 'Science of Religion.'" *Method and Theory in the Study of Religion*, vol. 16, pp. 205–33.

Saler, Benson. 2009. *Understanding Religion: Selected Essays*. Walter de Gruyter.

Saler, Benson. 2010. "Theory and Criticism: The Cognitive Science of Religion." *Method and Theory in the Study of Religion*, vol. 22, no. 4, pp. 330–9.

Saler, Benson. 2019. "Causality, Deconstruction, and an Unsettling Possibility." *Evolution, Cognition, and the History of Religions: A New Synthesis. Festschrift in Honour of Armin W. Geertz*, edited by Anders Klostergaard Petersen, Ingvild Sælid Gilhus, Luther H. Martin, Jeppe Sinding Jensen, and Jesper Sørensen, Brill, pp. 273–9.

Saler, Benson, Charles A. Ziegler, and Charles B. Moore. 1997. *UFO Crash at Roswell*. Smithsonian Institution Press.

Smith, Barbara Herrnstein. 2009. *Natural Reflections: Human Cognition at the Nexus of Science and Religion*. Yale University Press.

Vogt, Evon Z. 1972. "Comment on Benson Saler's Review of Zinacantan." *American Anthropologist*, vol. 74, no. 1–2, pp. 201–2.

PREFACE

In yesteryears the supernatural was accepted or believed in by many persons in Western societies. It continues to do so, as entertainment, as scholarship of one sort or another, and as much else. In brief, the supernatural is still with us, albeit in altered form here and there.

Furthermore, and I find this especially interesting, some themes and supernatural lifeways have not only expanded but have done so in a multitude of ways. Thus, for instance, some have done so without exhausting their basic identities (e.g., Bram Stokers "Dracula").

It seems to be very much the case that "Dracula" is, and for a number of years has been, a prime example of vampirism in North America. I judge it to be such in consequence of numerous citations not only of the novel but also of similarities in related phenomena (e.g., bookstores, art works, television scenarios).

This book contains four chapters describing the intellectual history of the supernatural in Euro-American cultures. In addition, I include two previously published articles, "Dracula and Carmilla" (Chapter 5) and "Towards a Realistic and Relevant Science of Religion" (Chapter 6). My goal is to provide an historical, philosophic, and cultural foundation toward the proposition of a scientific study of religion.

I register here my gratitude to the two editors, Luther H. Martin and Donald Wiebe, who helped me sort out various essays and much else.

ACKNOWLEDGMENTS

Thank you to the publishers for the permission to reprint the following chapters:

Chapter 5: Charles A. Ziegler and B. Saler 2005, "Dracula and Carmilla: Monsters and the Mind," *Philosophy and Literature*, vol. 29, no. 1: 217–27.

Chapter 6: Saler, B. 2004, "Towards a Realistic and Relevant 'Science of Religion.'" *Method and Theory in the Study of Religion*, vol. 16, no. 3:205–33 and republished with permission of Walter de Gruyter and Company, from 2009, *Understanding Religion: Selected Essays*, Benson Saler, vol. 48; permission conveyed through Copyright Clearance Center, Inc. This essay is a revised version of a lecture presented at a conference sponsored by the Universities of Turku and Åbo in April 2000. I am grateful to Professor Veikko Antonen and his colleagues at both universities for inviting me to Finland.[6]

This book by our friend and colleague Benson Saler is published posthumously, with final editing by Luther H. Martin and Donald Wiebe. We thank Professor Armin Geertz for contributing his appreciative insights into Saler's life and overview of his contributions to scholarship. We also thank Viswasirasini Govindarajan, Project Manager and her team of Integra Software Services, Pondicherry, India, and especially Sudha Soundrapandiyan, for their excellent copyediting of the volume and careful preparation of the index.

Introduction

This book touches on selected examples of the supernatural in Euro-American cultures. While many anthropologists and other students of religion have devoted numerous pages to arguments about the definition of religion, comparatively less interest has been lavished on the supernatural. Yet a serious argument can be made for paying greater attention to its intellectual history.

Among other things, a large number of Euro-American constructs invoking the supernatural are available to contemporary scholars. Some now consist largely of entertainment (e.g., vampires, werewolves, ghosts, spirits of the vasty deep, monsters, and so forth, albeit they occasionally serve more serious ends). Others, however, are profoundly serious but largely unknown in anthropological and related circles (e.g., a Roman Catholic theology of the supernatural that draws on the publications of Henri de Lubac [1967], Pierre Teilhard de Chardin [1960], and others).

Ideas about the supernatural typically arise out of diverse imaginings respecting the counterintuitive. Some of them constitute relatively unsystematized representations of enchanted worlds. Others, however, are institutionalized in popular religion and in statecraft. Thus, for example, classical Roman law mandated that the Senate investigate prodigies: objects or events held to surpass the normal course of nature. Such objects and events were studied by experts (mainly seers) who counseled the Senate as to whether or not they were omens (Beard et al. 1998).

The Latin expression *supra naturam excedens* (exceeding or surpassing nature) and the shorter expression *supra natura* were employed by the Romans as vocabulary resources for talking about phenomena deemed to be markedly unusual or unnatural. Those language resources, moreover, were eventually appropriated by Christian theologians in various ways. Thus, we note, a religious construct of the supernatural merged in Christian theology by at least the fifth century of the Common Era. We meet it in the Greek theological writings of St. Cyril of Alexandria (d. 444). Its most sophisticated formulations, however, are to be found in the literatures of scholasticism and in still later theological works, including some published in the twentieth century (e.g., Henri de Lubac, s.j., 1946; J. P. Kenney, s.j., 1972). As the Catholic Encyclopedia begins to describe it,

> The Supernatural Order is the ensemble of effects exceeding the powers of the created world gratuitously produced by God for the purpose of raising the rational creature above its native sphere to a God-like life and destiny. The meaning of the phrase fluctuates with that of its antithesis, the natural order.

Numbers of Christian theologians maintain that created human nature is supplemented by the supernatural gift of grace, a gratuity that is held to be superadded to created nature and that exceeds the power and dignity of created nature by rendering human salvation possible. Christian theologians, however, have debated whether or not god endowed human beings with a longing for grace when he originally created humankind. To suppose that he did, some theologians warn, would imply that the desire for grace—desire for a supernatural gift that only god can bestow—is an aspect of human nature. Such a claim, it has been argued, would compromise both the gratuity of grace and the absolute sovereignty of god (since, as a fully logical being, god would be obliged to provide the grace that he endowed in the longing for it).

This problem-set and the theological perspectives that it nurtures (e.g., the possibility that humankind is somehow open to grace rather than longing for it) constitute perhaps the most complex and subtle usage of the term "supernatural" in Christian theology. According to a Jesuit scholar who has published at some length on the supernatural, "the supernatural implies a new relationship, a fresh contact between God and man, a divine descent and union with a creature. Therefore, in the very concept of the supernatural in this strictest technical sense is implied the pre-existence of its term and of the Universe" (Kenny 1972:105).

Supernatural beliefs, both theistic and nontheistic, are virtually everywhere in the contemporary West. Such beliefs typically assert the existence and operation of agents and forces that many modern secular scholars deem beyond the ordinary course and possibilities of nature.

While contemporary scholars may accept the beliefs as "real" inasmuch as flesh-and-blood people entertain and express them, that is often not the case for the nature-transcending or counterintuitive phenomena that the beliefs affirm. Indeed, many modern secular scholars label beings and forces described or implied by such beliefs as "supernatural," and they call the beliefs that affirm them "supernatural beliefs."

The above-described practices reflect the modernist and secularist biases of many contemporary Western scholars of religion. We can appreciate those biases all the more when we compare them to the biases of numbers of European intellectuals in medieval and early modern times.

Thomas Aquinas, for instance, employs the Latin term *supernaturalis*, but he means by it something that comes from god alone.

Thomas would perhaps be shocked (and thereafter possibly bored) were he to watch reruns of the American television series "Supernatural," where a large diversity of sentient and non-sentient objects is credited with supernatural powers and identities.

Robert Bartlett (2008:20 ff.) calls our attention to certain intellectual consequences of the theological conviction that god—and god alone—can set aside or transcend natural laws. Some of what contemporary Euro-American religionists are likely to interpret as posited miracles or, more generally, as posited instantiations of the supernatural are, from Aquinas's point of view, falsely characterized. They are falsely characterized, that is, unless they are authored by god (who, Aquinas held, may sometimes perform miracles on behalf of saints or others). In the Thomist perspective, when creatures appear to be performing miracles on their own, their actions and the fruits of their labors ought not to be called supernatural. They are performed, according to Aquinas, "through some forces of natural things, although hidden from us, such as the miracles of demons, which are performed by magic arts" (Thomas Aquinas, quoted in Bartlett 2008: 20). Bartlett (2008) remarks that "[t]his idea that the demonic and the magical should be categorized as natural rather than supernatural was to have a long future, forming the cornerstone of conventional demonological thinking in the era of the great witch-hunt."

Bartlett cites Stuart Clark's impressive work, *Thinking with Demons: The Idea of Witchcraft in Early Modern Europe* (1997), in which Clark (1997:168–9) maintains that demonology was held by early modern Europeans to be "a form of natural knowledge" and that it is a mistake to associate the witchcraft beliefs of early modern Europeans with "supernaturalism" (Bartlett 2008:20).

Bartlett and Clark show us that some Europeans of yesteryear—at least some members of intellectual elites in their times and places (i.e., various schoolmen and various early modern European theorists)—were sharply restrictive in their figurations of the supernatural.

Many present-day Western academic students of religion widely attribute "supernatural beliefs" to numbers of other human populations.

But they do not always suppose that human populations who seem to hold such beliefs actually regard them as "supernatural." Two different examples of what I mean are provided by studies of ancient Greeks (discussed in Chapter 2) and Northern Ojibwa (discussed in Chapter 1).

According to a greatly respected student of the Northern Ojibwa, those Amerindians do not regard as "supernatural" various characters mentioned in their myths or stories, characters that many contemporary Euro-Americans would call supernatural. (The "ethnographic present" is the first half of the twentieth century and earlier.) The Northern Ojibwa do not regard such beings as supernatural, A. I. Hallowell (1960) tells us, because they lack a category of the "natural" and hence can have no category of the "supernatural." Lacking those categories, however, does not mean that they lack some concept and theory of causation. They appear to suppose that causation is intentional: that whatever happens in the universe happens because of human or human-like desire, will, and purpose, not because of impersonal causes.

And although ancient Greeks, unlike Northern Ojibwa, did categorize 'nature' (phusis), they (or numbers of them), according to some contemporary scholars (e.g., Werner Jaeger 1947; Dale Martin 2004), did not regard their gods as supernatural. Rather, they supposed that the gods and virtually everything else are part of nature (see Chapter 2).

In brief, while at least some Northern Ojibwa and some ancient Greeks (and legions of others) entertain and express beliefs of the sort that we call "supernatural," they do not maintain that those beliefs assert or affirm the existence of something "supernatural." They do not do so because, for one reason or another, they lack an explicit classificatory niche equivalent to our "supernatural." Nor, insofar as I can determine, does "supernatural" exist for them as a covert category or "cryptotype," an unlabeled but implicit classification presumably formed by the intersection of some of the semantic values constitutive of other categories. According to Dale Martin (2004), "the category of 'the supernatural' did not exist in ancient culture as a category." Indeed, supernatural is basically a Euro-American category in origin and in development.

Categories and Categorization

Uses of the word "supernatural" in contemporary Euro-American discourses support identifying that term as a category label. A category, broadly put, is a classificatory convention found among, or posited for, some human population. That is, it is a meaningful division or partition in a system of classifications. It affirms similarities and differences (Jackendoff 1983:77).

The English word "category" relates to a polysemous classical Greek verb, *katēgoréō*, meaning, among other things, to accuse or to predicate. That verb, moreover, is related to the verb *agoreúō*, to speak in public, and to the noun *agorá*, a marketplace and public assembly area where citizens gathered to conduct civic business.

As suggested above, an important aspect of categories is that they comprehend instantiations, even if in some cases the instantiations are entirely imaginary. "Unicorn," for instance, is a meaningful category for many persons in our society, and there is wide agreement about the distinctive features and/or the family resemblances of unicorns. But many who find the category meaningful deem it to be "empty" (devoid of existential instantiations) because "real" unicorns (living animals and fossils) have never existed. There are, nevertheless, numerous overlapping representations of unicorns in the graphic arts, in weavings, in literature, and elsewhere, and our analytical powers allow us to regard those imagined representations as instantiations of the category. That it may sometimes make ironic sense for us to do so is suggested by the fact that many readers of these lines can probably describe a unicorn more easily and (with respect to widespread Euro-American conventions) more accurately than they can describe an aardvark.

What is said of the category unicorn may, *mutatis mutandis*, be said of Euro-American theistic categories. But when we begin to analyze Euro-American god talk in different places and in different ages, we find significant differences in how deity was—and is—conceptualized. Thus, for instance, some contemporary Euro-Americans suppose the Judeo-Christian god to be "supernatural." If they were requested to justify that supposition, some might answer that, according to numbers of Jewish and Christian theologians, the Judeo-Christian god is uncreated, it is unconstrained in sovereignty, it is apart from nature, and it has powers that greatly surpass those within the natural realm. The ancient Greeks, in contrast, predicated some remarkable things of their gods but they did not describe those gods as supernatural. The Greek gods did not stand outside of nature (see Chapter 2). Indeed, they were sometimes described as having been generated by, or derived from, antecedent realities and as being beholden to causality in the form of their *moira*, their inexorable lot or portion, their destiny. In various texts (e.g., *The Iliad*), we note, the gods were depicted as neither omniscient nor omnipotent.

Regardless of how the ancient Greeks actually classified their gods, however, numbers of contemporary Euro-Americans may term those gods "supernatural." To some extent doing so may be a consequence of entertaining an inadequately explored and otherwise untested generalization: that most gods in most religions are "supernatural." But there are more particular reasons for why contemporary Westerners are likely to suppose that the Greek gods are supernatural. For one thing, of course, present-day Euro-Americans consciously employ a category of the supernatural, and it is often psychologically appealing to assimilate the relatively exotic to the relatively familiar. For another thing, some of us are probably influenced by the fact that several positive attributions credited to their gods by the ancient Greeks match some of the predicates that modern Euro-Americans associate with the category "supernatural." Thus, for example, the ancient Greek gods are immortal, they are ageless, they are invisible to human eyes (unless they choose to be seen), they drink and feast on substances reserved for the gods (nectar and ambrosia), and they are capable of investing mortals with godlike qualities. Indeed, numbers of present-day Westerners suppose in effect that ancient Greek beliefs about their gods conform to what contemporary

Euro-Americans generally mean by the expression "supernatural beliefs," even if supernatural was not a functionally significant category in ancient Greek cultural subjectivities.

Use of the Term "Supernatural" in the Study of Religion

Throughout the twentieth century many social scientists used the term "supernatural" in their descriptive, analytical, and theoretical works on religion. They often did so without apparent concern for the probity or propriety of such usages. But a minority of their fellow social scientists—Émile Durkheim (1915), A. Irving Hallowell (1960), Godfrey Lienhardt (1961), Benson Saler (1977), Robin Horton (1983), Morton Klass (1995), and others—explicitly protested what they took to be facile uses of the term "supernatural" in descriptions of non-Western beliefs. They warned against imposing a natural/supernatural opposition on the ideations of peoples who may not entertain that distinction.

Natural is the quality or condition of pertaining to nature (connotatively without artifice). The above-mentioned social scientists more or less conceived of nature as a realm governed by impersonal and inflexible laws. That concept of nature, various ethnographers report—I cite Hallowell (1960) above for the Northern Ojibwa—is absent in the intellectual traditions of numbers of non-Western peoples. Strictly speaking, moreover—or so Durkheim (1965[1915]) maintained—it is also absent in the writings of the greatest thinkers of Western classical antiquity.

Durkheim, Hallowell, and like-minded others, furthermore, supposed that peoples who lack the idea of an impersonal natural order that operates according to necessity also lack our conceptualization of the supernatural as a domain of imagined exceptions to the natural order. To impose our natural-supernatural opposition on the perspectives and beliefs of such peoples, they held, would therefore misrepresent the cultural subjectivities of those on whom it is imposed. It would constitute an egregious case of ethnocentrism. Supernatural, some scholars advised, should be reserved for cases where a natural/supernatural opposition is actually entertained by the people studied. Certain other twentieth-century scholars, however, as I point out in Chapter 1, explicitly disagreed with that advice.

Matters can become even more complex if one attempts to follow the seemingly similar but actually different advice of Melford E. Spiro and Luther H. Martin. Spiro maintains that he wants to avoid muddying the waters with metaphysical statements, and so he will write about superhuman religious figures rather than supernatural ones. Martin (personal communication) starts off by making a seemingly straightforward and, in principle, testable claim: that "[w]hile all supernatural agents are superhuman, not all superhuman agents are supernatural." We are confronted, moreover, by complexities that Martin, a noted scholar of ancient religions, deems important: such matters, for instance, as the loci attributed to the gods of ancient religions (Did the votaries of those ancient gods suppose that the gods lived in our world or in hypercosmic space, and how does an answer to that question relate to whether or not the ancient gods were superhuman or were held to be supernatural?)

Natural and Cultural

In the twenty-first century the word "supernatural" continues to be utilized widely in descriptions of non-Western beliefs, but relatively few voices are now raised in criticism (for some examples, however, see a special issue of the journal *Anthropological Forum*, vol. 13, no. 2, 2003). Many (probably most) contemporary social scientists apply that term without apparent concern for the caveats of yesteryear. Indeed, in the cognitive science of religion it is rare to see such warnings cited, let alone discussed. In that approach to religion, moreover, the term "natural" is often strongly foregrounded.

While predecessors treated the natural as a sort of background constant to be contrasted to the supernatural, numbers of contemporary scholars who draw upon the cognitive, neural, and evolutionary sciences treat the natural as itself a near ultimate object of scholarly investigation in religious studies. Their emphasis is on human nature, actualities, and potentialities deemed natural because they are held to inhere in being human and because, when they find expression, their expression is neither crucially nor mainly learned responses to stimuli (albeit expression may be culturally colored).

Now, the distinguished intellectual historian Arthur O. Lovejoy (1935:12) opines that the word "nature" "is probably the most equivocal in the vocabulary of the European peoples." We may therefore expect to encounter significant differences in uses of the English terms "nature" and "natural" and in applications of cognate expressions in other Euro-American languages. That is indeed the case in the academic study of religion. Thus, for example, to enlarge on what I pointed out earlier, some scholars rest their ideas of the natural on the understanding that "the phenomena of the universe are bound together by necessary relations, called laws" (Durkheim 1965 [1915]:41), whereas others affirm that in the explanatory efforts of the cognitive science of religion, "natural" typically means that "the activity in question (mental or motor) arises through the course of ordinary development without special cultural support" (Barrett 2010:169). Indeed, in the contemporary cognitive science of religion (CSR) a great deal of attention devolves on a contrast between the natural and the cultural.

Interest in pursuing a nature-culture contrast relates to overarching intellectual perspectives and commitments among proponents of the cognitive science of religion. That is, it celebrates both "methodological" and "ontological" naturalism. As Jason Blum (2011) succinctly points out, the former endorses and seeks to emulate or incorporate the methods and theories of the natural sciences while the latter denies existence to postulated supernatural causations. In working toward the development of a naturalistic science of religion, moreover, the theorizing of many proponents of CSR, when compared to that of numbers of earlier academic students of religion, circumscribes or reduces the causal significance of culture in accounting for the human condition.

An emphasis on a natural/cultural opposition is by no means new. The current conceptualization owes something, I think, to Lévi-Strauss's structuralist opposition between nature and culture and to other nature/culture partitions in anthropology. The general opposition, moreover, owes something to older analogs in philosophy and theology, going back at least as far as Aristotle's distinctions between *phúsis* (nature) and *téchnē* (art) and *phúsis* and *nómos* (human law, custom). What is relatively new in CSR theorizing (or, at any rate, worth remarking) is the strategic assimilation of the opposition into contemporary Darwinian perspectives on the human condition. Among other things, that assimilation helps correct what I regard as an unfortunate proclivity traditionally evinced by many of my fellow anthropologists: the investiture of culture with powers and importance that go beyond compelling attributions. But, as sometimes happens in corrective movements, the pendulum occasionally swings too far in the other direction, and some proponents of the cognitive science of religion, in my opinion, do not always accord culture the attention and significance that it deserves.

Natural and Supernatural

In the course of this book, I consider different senses of the natural as they may or may not nurture some contrastive sense of the supernatural. As remarked earlier, while "natural" does not necessarily imply "supernatural," supernatural does imply some concept of the natural. An inquiry into the intellectual history of the supernatural is unavoidably an inquiry into the intellectual history of the natural.

The term "supernatural"—as in the important theoretical and analytical expression "supernatural agents"—is sometimes employed in CSR as, in part, a gloss for "unreal" or "counter-factual." It is typically applied to conceptualized entities or forces that combine intuitive and counterintuitive elements, the latter denoting what modern Western scholars take to be supernatural (Barrett 2011; Boyer 1994, 2001; Pyysiäinen 2001; Saler 2009:13–14). We cannot, however, affirm a simple correspondence between the counterintuitive and the supernatural inasmuch as there are some challenges to such a generalization. (The most arresting, in my opinion, are the highly counterintuitive but nonsupernatural concepts and constructs of modern physics.) Yet although there is not a simple correspondence between the counterintuitive and the supernatural, there is an important correspondence nevertheless.

Proponents of the current cognitive science of religion generally hold that beliefs about "supernatural agents" are to significant extents products or by-products of panhuman dispositions established in the course of human evolution. Although such beliefs are likely to take on cultural colorations, they are also likely to be underdetermined by culture. They are, in short, "natural" in that they do not exclusively or mainly depend on learning and on extensive informational downloading when transmitted across generations (see, for example, one of the foundational texts in CSR, Pascal Boyer's *The Naturalness of Religious Ideas*, 1994; see also Robert N. McCauley's *Why Religion Is Natural and Science Is Not*, 2011). This perhaps accounts for why CSR theorists are seemingly untroubled in their uses of the term "supernatural." The universality of dispositions that nurture supernaturalist imaginings, they might say if prodded, justifies their wide use of the term "supernatural."

Current CSR discussions that include uses of the terms "natural" and "supernatural" can be further illuminated by being viewed within the context of a related shift in scholarly emphasis, one that is not thoroughgoing but is nevertheless discernible. While numbers of pre-CSR studies were informed by assumptions about panhuman conditions undergirding cultural diversity, they were also very sensitive to, and very appreciative of, that diversity. They sought to describe the different subjectivities of the peoples studied. More recent studies, at least among scholars with strong evolutionary and cognitive commitments, tend to emphasize human commonalities, especially as they illumine and are illuminated by a theory of mind. This is not to say that these scholars are uninterested in human differences. But in recognizing cultural differences, they tend to view such differences as mutually supported by, and mutually supportive of, panhuman inference systems and other universal cognitive structures and mechanisms presumably established in the course of human evolution.

Observations

The materials available for exploring applications of the terms "natural" and "supernatural" are so diverse and rich that I can only sample them in a work of reasonable length. That is why the word "observation" is so important. Observations need not be exhaustive; they may well be (and usually are) fragmentary. Nor need they be lineally coherent, one following genealogically from another. They may only—as in this work—relate to some of the high points in complex stories. I hope, however, that what I do include will help cast light, directly or indirectly, on certain issues in the study of religions and religion.

My samplings of a complex history may strike some readers as less than optimal, and critics may prefer a different set of choices. Fair enough!

I am of the opinion, nevertheless, that although I might have discussed Y instead of X, or N instead of M, the overall drift of what I conclude would be more or less the same. Unlike Durkheim, for instance, I do not conclude that the emergence of the popular category of the supernatural is "a conquest of the positive sciences."

Fortunately, we can trace the course of various Greek and Latin *huper* and supra compounds that play some role in the story of the supernatural (e.g., *huperousios*, beyond substance; *hupernous*, beyond mind; and *huperphues*, beyond nature). In brief, we can trace some of the seeds from which our supernatural grew long before the emergence of the so-called positive sciences in early modern Europe. And thereon, I think, rests a tale worth telling, if only in part.

1

Social Scientists and the Supernatural

The views of social scientists respecting uses of the term "supernatural" gravitate toward three discernible positions:

(1) A small minority maintains that social scientists should avoid using the term "supernatural" in describing beliefs unless the believers themselves entertain a distinction between the natural and the supernatural that resembles our popular distinction. (2) Some social scientists who are familiar with the cautionary arguments made by persons in the first group explicitly reject those arguments. They assert that it is meaningful to talk about supernatural entities and forces in the case of some Euro-American beliefs and that it is meaningful, convenient, and not critically misleading to apply the term "supernatural" to analogous entities and forces in the beliefs of non-Western peoples. They agree that members of non-Western societies may not entertain the same ideas about nature and causality that we do, but, they argue, that need not interdict use of the term "supernatural" by analogy. (3) Many social scientists both use the term "supernatural" and are mute respecting the arguments advanced by members of the other two groups. They may or may not be familiar with those arguments. If the former is the case, their seemingly untroubled use of the term can be taken

as implying disagreement with members of the first group, a disagreement that they do not otherwise assert. In any case, these social scientists use the term "supernatural" without explicit justification. They apply the expression "supernatural beliefs" as a label for what they often deem to be false beliefs.

In this chapter, I summarize the views of selected social scientists who can be sorted into one of the three analytically posited groups described above. I begin with Durkheim.

Émile Durkheim (1858–1917)

Émile Durkheim's *The Elementary Forms of the Religious Life* was published in French in 1912, and its first English translation appeared in 1915. Many social scientists, I think, would agree that it is one of the most influential works ever published by one of their number. It addresses a variety of issues, and its appeal is multifaceted. Durkheim not only attempts to characterize and define religion by analyzing what he supposes to be the most elementary form of religion now known (that is, the religion of certain Australian Aborigines), but he makes a more general case for interpreting various aspects of human life as symbolic expressions of underlying social facts. He draws the reader's attention to "collective representations" as important features of human cultures (and as analytical and theoretical alternatives to Kantian postulations of innate ideas). Along with an earlier work that he coauthored with Marcel Mauss (Durkheim and Mauss 1963 [1903]), moreover, he offers us a perspective on categories and classifications that is worth considering. In a variety of ways, indeed, the 1912 book stimulates our thinking about social science and religion.

In writing his book, Durkheim makes use of a ploy that many authors have utilized in attempting to bolster their theories. Early on, that is, Durkheim attacks points of view alternative to his own respecting the nature, origins, and persistence of religion. One by one he attempts to demolish rival theories, thereby, perhaps, softening up the reader for the acceptance of his own theory when, at last, he presents it. Thus, for instance, Durkheim attacks definitions or characterizations of religion that accord crucial importance to the idea of the supernatural.

By "supernatural," Durkheim (1965:39) writes, "is understood all sorts of things which surpass the limits of our knowledge; the supernatural is the world of the mysterious, of the unknowable, of the un-understandable." He maintains, however, that this sense of mystery "is not of primitive origin" (1965:43). For so-called primitive persons, Durkheim supposes, the universe is neither complex nor mysterious. "It is science and not religion," Durkheim avers, "which has taught men that things are complex and difficult to understand" (1965:42).

It is our recently acquired understanding of "the immutability and the inflexibility of the order of things" (1965:41), Durkheim claims, that disposes us to deem posited exceptions as being marvelous and mysterious. Indeed, "in order to arrive at the idea of the supernatural," Durkheim insists, things so labeled must be conceived of as being "impossible"—"that is to say, irreconcilable with an order which, rightly or wrongly, appears to us to be implied in the nature of things" (1965:43). In sum, Durkheim maintains, "[i]n order to say that certain things are supernatural, it is necessary to have the sentiment that a natural order of things exists, that is to say, that the phenomena of the universe are bound together by necessary relations, called laws" (1965:41).

The idea of a necessary order, Durkheim tells us, has been constructed by the modern positive sciences. The contrary idea, the idea of the supernatural "as we understand it," is dependent on it and thus of relatively recent origin. "Even the greatest thinkers of classical antiquity," Durkheim claims, "never succeeded in becoming fully conscious of it" (1965:41). Inasmuch as the supernatural is not a universal concept, Durkheim concludes, we cannot base a universal definition of religion on it.

Durkheim imagines that the entities and forces in which so-called primitive peoples believe, although different from those recognized by modern science, are for such peoples "no more unintelligible than are gravitation and electricity for the physicist of today" (1965:40). Even though those forces are typically thought of "under the form of spiritual beings or conscious wills," recourse to personal agency rather than to impersonal forces, while intellectually consequential, is not by itself an indication of irrationality. That is because "[t]he reason has no repugnance a priori to admitting that the so-called inanimate bodies should be directed by intelligences" (1965:40). But once people recognize that "the phenomena of the universe are bound together by necessary relations called laws," Durkheim maintains, whatever is contrary to those laws must strike proponents of the laws as impossible and irrational, for those laws express "the manner in which things are logically related," and such laws do not admit of exceptions (1965:41).

To put all of this in sharper focus: The idea of the supernatural, according to Durkheim, cannot be found in societies that lack the understanding of nature supported by the positive sciences. Put another way, the idea of the supernatural can only be found in societies that endorse the view of nature that Durkheim attributes to the modern positive sciences. Historically then, Durkheim writes, the supernatural is "a conquest of the positive sciences" (1965:41).

The supernatural, Durkheim tells us, refers to posited exceptions to the operation of the universal laws that govern nature. Such exceptions, from the standpoint of the positive sciences as Durkheim describes them, are conceptual but not actual. Actual exceptions are impossible because those sciences hold that nature admits of no exceptions. Ascribing actuality to conceptualized exceptions would therefore be simultaneously false to nature as the positive sciences conceive it and subversive of the intellectual support accorded those sciences.

As We Understand It

To pursue the matter further, there is the phrase "as we understand it" in Durkheim's characterization of the idea of the supernatural. Who are the "we" in his affirmation, and what do we (or they) understand?

The "we" whom Durkheim probably had in mind constituted an intellectual subclass in France and in other Western countries in 1912. Members, we may suppose, would be relatively educated persons whose conceptions of the order of things owed much to late-nineteenth-century and early-twentieth-century classical Euro-American physics. Such persons would be more likely than other members of their societies to support philosophical monism, the idea that all events and forces in the universe are to be explained naturalistically. That monism contrasts to philosophical dualism, the idea that while many things are to be explained naturalistically, some other things are to be accounted for super naturalistically. Super naturalistically in this case relates to the Oxford English Dictionary's first definition of "supernatural": "That is above nature; belonging to a higher realm or system than that of nature; transcending the powers or the ordinary course of nature."

While we can readily appreciate how Durkheim's characterization of the "impossible" may satisfy philosophical monists, what about philosophical dualists? Many of the latter in France and in other countries generally maintained, and numbers continue to maintain, that one must account for certain things super naturalistically because some affirmations of the supernatural are true or likely or perhaps mainly desirable even if they are "un-understandable" or "mysterious" or even seemingly "impossible."

It appears that Durkheim's explication of the supernatural is most coherent—which is to say, least in need of nuancing—when viewed in polar opposition to the anti-supernatural beliefs of atheists who are uncompromisingly grounded in the positive sciences. Such people are very likely to dismiss beliefs in the supernatural as false beliefs. For them, supernatural in effect means erroneous.

Durkheim fails to account directly for why some of the fellow citizens of modern philosophical monists invest belief in the reality or logicality or desirability of the supernatural. But based on his characterization of the supernatural, we may infer that, in his opinion, those contemporary Euro-Americans who profess some form of supernaturalism lack an appreciation of "the immutability and the inflexibility of the order of things" that is both thoroughgoing and exclusive.

The Idea of the Impossible

To reiterate Durkheim's central claim (1965:43): "In order to arrive at the idea of the supernatural," entities, events, or forces so labeled must be conceived to be "impossible"—that is, conceived to be "irreconcilable with an order which, rightly or wrongly, appears to us to be implied in the nature of things." Such a characterization of the impossible, as I pointed out, accords with philosophical monism. In the strictest sense of the understandings set forth by Durkheim, the impossible does not and cannot occur or exist. Hence from the strict positivist's point of view, affirmations of the supernatural are the affirmations of errors. If the errors persist, they do so as superstitions or as illusions or, worse, as delusions.

When we turn to *Webster's Ninth New Collegiate Dictionary*, we find that a primary meaning listed for "impossible" is "incapable of being or of occurring." That meaning suits the philosophical monist. But it need not—nor did it, nor does it—discomfort all philosophical dualists.

Some dualists may appear to endorse our dictionary definition of the impossible while adding that certain things that seem impossible do nevertheless occur or exist and that that is what is acutely "wonderful"— or perhaps even "miraculous"—about the supernatural. Furthermore, "impossible" has been invoked paradoxically on occasion in support of the putative authority of extraordinary claims, as, for instance, in these lines of Tertullian written about 206 CE:

> The Son of God was crucified; it is not shameful because it must be shameful. And the Son of God died: it is believable because it can't be grasped. And having been entombed, he arose. It is certain because it is impossible.
>
> (*De Carne Christi* V.4)

Dualists may even seem to reap discursive benefits on occasion from claiming that while many things are impossible, certain putatively impossible things actually do occur. Such claims may sometimes dramatically frame the endorsement of a larger claim, one that many persons, numbers of monists included, are likely to accept: that human life confronts us with paradox (and by so doing inevitably defeats the monist's desire for thoroughgoing consistency and coherence).

Durkheim's Supernatural and So-Called Primitive Peoples

Now, in the preceding pages I have been concerned with ideas and perspectives as they may occur in Euro-American or "Western" societies. That concern is salient throughout this work. In places, however, attention is directed to the beliefs and classificatory structures of so-called primitive peoples. "Primitive peoples," classically, are nonliterate persons who live in small-scale societies and participate in non-Western cultures. References to scholarly claims about such populations, I hope, will prove useful in foregrounding what is involved in Western constructions of the supernatural. To that end, in addition to considering certain of the views of Durkheim, I also explore some of the views of two other scholars: the French historian of philosophy Lucien Lévy-Bruhl and the American cultural anthropologist A. Irving Hallowell.

Both Lévy-Bruhl and Hallowell accept Durkheim's claim that supernatural implies a contrast with the natural. Both, moreover, in effect agree with Durkheim in supposing that the "impossible" as Durkheim characterizes it is absent in the ideations of so-called primitives. Lévy-Bruhl agrees explicitly. Hallowell agrees implicitly when he maintains that the Northern Ojibwa do not entertain a natural-supernatural distinction because they lack a sense of the "natural" that is based on the operation of impersonal laws.

Lucien Lévy-Bruhl (1857–1939)

Lévy-Bruhl is famous among anthropologists for claiming that a "primitive mentality" exists and that it differs in significant respects from what he broadly takes to be modern Euro-American mentality. Lévy-Bruhl's formulation of a basic and behaviorally consequential difference in mentalities constitutes a disagreement with the views of certain late-nineteenth-century and early-twentieth-century scholars who constituted the so-called English School of Anthropology. Edward Burnett Tylor, the author of *Primitive Culture* (1871), is their most influential theorist. Tylor argues in favor of the psychic unity of humankind. That is, while maintaining that so-called primitive peoples sometimes reason from ill-chosen and faulty premises, Tylor nevertheless holds that such peoples are cognitively similar to us and may for the most part be deemed rational as we conventionally understand rationality. Lévy-Bruhl disagrees, although the substance and intensity of his disagreement vary somewhat over the years (for some of the details, see Cazeneuve 1972 [1963]; Keck 2008; and Saler 1997, reprinted in Saler 2009).

Lévy-Bruhl's first book on "primitive mentality" was published in 1910. By the time of his death in 1939 he had published an additional five books addressed to that topic. Following the Second World War, eleven of his notebooks—preparations, probably, for a seventh book—were discovered and published. His most extensive treatment of the supernatural occurs in his fourth book, *Le surnaturel et la nature dans la mentalité primitive*. Published in 1931, it appeared in an English translation in 1936 under the title *Primitives and the Supernatural*.

Early in his fourth book, Lévy-Bruhl remarks that "although primitives can clearly differentiate things that appear supernatural from those that occur in the ordinary course of nature, they rarely imagine them as separate, for in them 'the sense of the impossible' is lacking" (1936:5). In a later passage, Lévy-Bruhl (1936:34) declares that even though "primitive man" may not confuse the worlds of the supernatural and the natural "in their essence," it is often the case "that he does not differentiate between them."

In these passages, Lévy-Bruhl seems both to accept Durkheim's views and to distance himself from them. That is, he agrees that in the strictest sense (i.e., in the Durkheimian sense) an explicit category of the supernatural is absent among "primitives" owing to the absence of a sense of the impossible comparable to Durkheim's sense of the impossible. Yet such peoples, according to Lévy-Bruhl, nevertheless have the intellectual power to "clearly differentiate" between "things that appear supernatural" and those that "occur in the ordinary course of nature," albeit they often fail to distinguish between them. While this may suggest to some readers a distinction between what "primitive" peoples can do and what they usually do, more is involved, and further explication seems desirable.

From his first book in 1910 through the sixth book and the posthumously published *Notebooks*, Lévy-Bruhl draws our attention to what he calls a "mystical orientation," an orientation that he deems an important component or aspect of the so-called primitive mentality. That orientation, basically, is an orientation to the presence, actions, or traces of suprasensible realities, realities not immediately accessible to the ordinary workings of our senses—gods, ghosts, spirits, and the like. In his early books Lévy-Bruhl pictures "primitives" as heavily committed to the mystical, in notable contrast to Westerners whom he supposes to be more marked by attachments to the commonsensical. In his later works, however, he blurs the contrast somewhat. He claims that he has long believed that contemporary Western populations give significant weight to the mystical. And he explicitly allows that "primitives" make room for the commonsensical. But, Lévy-Bruhl insists, a real and consequential contrast between "primitive peoples" and modern Euro-Americans can nevertheless be drawn, for the former are more absorbed in the mystical than the latter.

While in his first three books Lévy-Bruhl gives us grounds for supposing that "primitive" peoples do not operate with a distinctive category of the supernatural, in his fourth book that is not the case. In the fourth book Lévy-Bruhl treats the suprasensible realities affirmed by "primitives" as instantiations of what he calls "the affective category of the supernatural." There are, however, certain subtleties that we ought to note. In affirming the importance of a category of the supernatural among so-called primitive peoples Lévy-Bruhl does not claim that those peoples consciously recognize and name the category. Nevertheless, by asserting the implicit existence and operation of such a category, Lévy-Bruhl breaks with a strict conformance to Durkheim's views. He does so, I think, not because he wants to emphasize the supernatural character of instantiations of the category. Rather, he wants to impress on the reader the affective significance of the category. He employs "supernatural" as a convenient descriptive term that most readers can handle. As a convenience, it does not steal attention away from what he emphasizes: the claim that the category of the supernatural among "primitive peoples" is not so much intellectual or cognitive as it is emotional.

The affective category of the supernatural is an analytical construct that directs our attention to the role of affectivity in thought. Lévy-Bruhl points out that his philosophically minded Euro-American predecessors and contemporaries tend to distinguish among the "emotional," the "motor," and the "intellectual" aspects of human life. But that classificatory edifice, he opines, is not serviceable for attending to the ideas of "primitive" peoples. In the "primitive mentality," Lévy-Bruhl avers, affectivity so permeates or colors thought that many ideas are more "felt" than "thought."

Lévy-Bruhl cautions us not to regard the collective representations of "primitives" as exclusively or even primarily intellectual. They are in great degree affective, especially and preeminently when they posit unseen entities and forces. Imagining supra-sensible realities, and responding to what is imagined, answers to emotional needs and dispositions.

Furthermore, in claiming (especially in his later works) that a mystical mentality is discernible to some degree in all human minds, Lévy-Bruhl suggests that Western thought is also sometimes colored by affectivity. If we accept his suggestion, then we may conclude, as does Lévy-Bruhl, that a purely intellectualist approach to modern Euro-American thought would also be inadequate.

A. Irving Hallowell (1892–1974)

Although numbers of young anthropologists today may know little or nothing about Hallowell, he was once a greatly respected figure within the anthropological profession. Famous in his own time for his solid and innovative work as judged against the standards then applicable, he was influential in the development of a number of subfields or academic specialties: in culture and personality studies, in the cross-cultural use of the Rorschach Test, in ethnohistorical and ethnographic studies of North American Indians (his own major fieldwork was among Northern Ojibwa along the Berens River in Manitoba, supplemented by work among Ojibwa in Lac du Flambeau, Wisconsin), in developing an informed phylogenetic perspective on the emergence of human culture and behavior, in asking and attempting to answer questions about what it means to be human, and in his explorations of the meanings of category labels (e.g., "property") employed as descriptive and analytical terms in cross-cultural research. His contributions to the last listed specialty are particularly relevant to the subject matter of this book.

Hallowell held that various "weasel words"—an expression that I heard him voice on a number of occasions—are sometimes carelessly invoked by anthropologists in ethnographic research and in ethnographic monographs, thereby misrepresenting the cultural subjectivities of the non-Western populations among whom anthropologists work. One such word, he claimed, is "supernatural."

Hallowell's major published statement on the term "supernatural" is found in a 1960 essay, "Ojibwa Ontology, Behavior, and World View." In that paper Hallowell claims that to describe characters in Northern Ojibwa myths as supernatural would be "completely misleading, if for no other reason than the fact that the concept of 'supernatural' presupposes a concept of the 'natural'. The latter," he holds, "is not present in Ojibwa thought" (1960:28). That is, the Ojibwa do not suppose that the universe operates in accordance with impersonal laws. Rather, it is filled with, and it is driven by, intelligence, will, purpose, desire, and communicative abilities of one sort or another. As Hallowell puts it,

> With respect to the Ojibwa conception of causality, all my own observations suggest that a culturally constituted psychological set operates which inevitably directs the reasoning of individuals towards an explanation of events in personalistic terms. Who did it, who is responsible, is always the crucial question to be answered.
>
> (1960:44–5)

Hallowell's generalization about "the Ojibwa conception of causality" relates to a larger generalization. "Although not formally abstracted and articulated philosophically," he writes, the nature of "persons" is the focal point of Ojibwa ontology and the key to the psychological unity and dynamics of their world outlook. This aspect of their metaphysics of being permeates the content of their cognitive processes: perceiving, remembering, imagining, conceiving, judging, and reasoning.

According to Hallowell, the universe conceptualized by his informants is populated by sentient beings, by "persons," among whom human beings are but one type of person. Because, as he understands it, the Ojibwa lack a concept of a natural order that turns on impersonal laws, Hallowell is unwilling to apply the adjective supernatural to the nonhuman agents whom they recognize (1960:28). Instead, he calls them "other-than-human" beings or persons in an effort to minimize distortion in his descriptions of Ojibwa subjectivities.

Hallowell opines, moreover, that "[i]t is unfortunate that the natural-supernatural dichotomy has been so persistently invoked by many anthropologists in describing the outlook of peoples in cultures other than our own" (1960:28). That dichotomy, he holds, should be invoked only when it can be shown that the population to which it is applied operates with a distinction similar to the distinction entertained in our cultural subjectivity. That point, together with others that I cite here in my discussion of Hallowell, constitutes an endorsement—an endorsement grounded in ethnographic fieldwork—of Durkheim's general argument about the meaning and limited utility of the term "supernatural."

It is worth pointing out that Hallowell does not endorse the surely untrue general notion that the absence of a word reliably indicates the absence of a corresponding concept or phenomenon. Nor is he opposed in principle to using Euro-American terms and constructs for analytical and theoretical purposes. Thus, for example, he knows that some non-Western populations have no distinct term for, or concept of, what we call "religion," yet he does not object when ethnographers write about the religions of such peoples. But in aspiring to describe the cultural subjectivities of non-Western populations, as noted earlier, one must pay attention to how the people themselves, as Tylor puts it, "classify out the world." In doing so, many anthropologists contend (even if they do not always follow their own prescription), one ought to guard against the facile application of Euro-American descriptive terms that would obscure or distort what is actually important in native reckonings.

In Hallowell's opinion, to re-state a quotation given earlier, "the nature of 'persons' is the focal point of Ojibwa ontology and the key to the psychological unity and dynamics of their world outlook." The importance of that understanding would be compromised or subverted, Hallowell holds, were we to speak of Ojibwa "supernaturalism." Indeed, he objects to applying the term "supernatural" in the Ojibwa case not simply because it implicates what the Ojibwa lack—a conceptualized division whereby some things pertain to a realm of impersonal causality called "the natural" and other things pertain to a realm outside of the natural—but also because such an implication runs counter to the salient and seemingly thorough going attribution of causal powers to a multiplicity of "persons," a multiplicity of agents, among the Ojibwa.

From an Ojibwa point of view as presented by Hallowell, moreover, human agents not only overlap in various ways with other-than-human agents, but it can sometimes prove difficult to tell them apart. According to Hallowell's informants, both human and nonhuman agents may have powers of metamorphosis. Human sorcerers, for example, may turn into bears, and bears may turn into humans. As Hallowell understands it, "[o]utward appearance" among the Ojibwa "is only an incidental attribute of being" (1960:35) and "neither animal nor human characteristics define categorical differences in the core of being" (1960:35). "What persists and gives continuity to being" in Ojibwa understandings, Hallowell tells us, "is the vital part, or soul" (1960:38). In sum, the Ojibwa worldview, as Hallowell describes it, not only emphasizes personal causality, but it calls attention to "the deceptiveness of appearances" (1960:40). This, I think, could be interpreted as an ancillary reason for being chary about invoking our natural/supernatural distinction in describing Ojibwa cultural subjectivities.

Analogy and Approximation

As mentioned earlier, some scholars hold that we can responsibly use the term "supernatural" in describing the contents of non-Western beliefs when those beliefs are thought to be analogous to, or when they are held to approximate to, Euro-American beliefs commonly said to have a "supernatural" content. We can do so, they maintain, without having to demonstrate that the believers entertain a concept of nature akin to our concept of nature. That viewpoint runs counter to the positions taken by Durkheim, Hallowell, Lévy-Bruhl, and various others. But before further considering it, some discussion of what may be meant by analogy and approximation can be useful.

An analogy posits a similarity in two or more things that are otherwise recognized to be different. Approximation is the state or condition of coming near or being similar to something else. As in the case of analogies, things that are said to approximate to one another are not deemed identical or fully overlapping; rather, their similarity or nearness is judged to be imperfect.

While writing definitions of analogy and approximation may seem easy, there are difficulties attendant on applications of the root notion of "similarity" that need to be considered. In a thought-provoking essay, the philosopher Nelson Goodman describes what he calls seven "strictures" on similarity (1972:437–46). Goodman argues that an abstract, universal conception of similarity cannot be meaningfully achieved, for the truth about similarity is that it is "relative, variable, [and] culture-dependent" (1972:438). Were we to attempt to escape its relativity, variability, and dependency, we would be stymied by the fact that any two things could be said to resemble one another in a virtual infinity of ways—and, indeed, any two things could also be said to differ in a virtual infinity of ways. Goodman (1972:437) pens an arresting remark: "Similarity, I submit, is insidious." I suspect, however, that the seeming blatancy of Goodman's remark has contributed to an over-reading of him on the part of some.

Goodman does not reject all efforts to establish similarity. He is aware that people in their work-a-day lives deem objects or events to be similar or different, that they commonly talk about things as being like or unlike other things, and that such talk is meaningful and useful for them. Indeed, Goodman explicitly allows that similarity may be clear enough "when closely confined by context and circumstance in ordinary discourse," but the point that he wants to make is that "it is hopelessly ambiguous when torn loose" (1972:444).

I regard Goodman's essay as insightful and valuable. But I hasten to append three observations respecting it. First, Goodman's seven strictures address what the developmental psychologist Linda B. Smith (1993:217) calls "philosophers' worries." She herself appears to have a worry about such worries, for she writes that "[o]ne danger in letting the philosophers' worries set the research agenda ... is that we may forget the psychology of similarity." Smith's own psychological research on similarity leads her to suppose that there is "a unitary concept of sameness that transcends specific perceptual features" (1993:223). Smith holds, moreover, that the philosopher Goodman worried that similarity is "incoherent." But if he did, Smith opines, it was a good kind of coherence.

Second, in addition to impressive experimental work in psychology dealing with similarity (for reviews see Smith 1993, and Gentner and Rattermann 1991), some psychologists and philosophers have been critical of Goodman's treatment of the subject (for a more recent review see Decock and Douven 2011). Much of Goodman's essay, in my reading of it, strikes me as congruent with, and an enrichment of, philosophical points that Goodman makes in earlier publications. Thus, for instance, sixteen years before the essay on similarity Goodman declares that his endorsement of nominalism "consists specifically in the refusal to recognize classes" (Goodman 1956:16–17), a refusal that would seem all the more sensible were we to agree that similarity, the very concept that supports the idea of classes, is itself incoherent. Goodman's essay on similarity may be more complex and subtle than some readers suppose, and it could best be read within the context of Goodman's philosophical oeuvre. In any case, not all of the points that he affirms in the similarity essay are accepted as definitive by all specialists.

Third and finally, regardless of our position on larger philosophical issues respecting similarity, family resemblance, and (dare I say it?) the like, we are obliged to deal with the fact that many anthropologists and others deem some of the beliefs of non-Western peoples to resemble Western beliefs about the "supernatural"—so much so, indeed, that they extend the term "supernatural" to those non-Western beliefs, the different caveats of Émile Durkheim, A. I. Hallowell, Lucien Lévy-Bruhl, and Nelson Goodman notwithstanding.

Analogy and Convenience

Social scientists as varied as the North American cultural anthropologist Marvin Harris (1975:514), the British social anthropologist Maurice Hocart (1932a:59–61, 1932b), and the Swedish cultural anthropologist Åke Hultkrantz (1979 [1967]:10, n.2; 1983) advocate using the word "supernatural" in ethnographic and ethnological publications—using it by analogy in the case of Harris and Hocart and using it for analogy and something more in the case of Hultkrantz. All three explicitly sanction applying the term "supernatural" to beings and forces conceived of by non-Westerners when such conceptualizations resemble those that Euro-Americans label "supernatural." These anthropologists, moreover, are seemingly untroubled by strictures of the kinds affirmed by Nelson Goodman. In fact, their judgments of similarity may even strike us as being sanctioned to some extent by Goodman's allowance for culture-dependent judgments that are "closely confined by context and circumstance in ordinary discourse."

By describing analogous ideas and beliefs as supernatural in content, Harris and Hocart suggest, we flag in terms meaningful to us what we regard as interesting. Doing so, they note, is convenient in connecting to Western audiences. Western academics usually write for, and lecture to, Western audiences. And those audiences commonly find talk of the supernatural to be meaningful and attention-getting.

Hultkrantz, however, goes further than Hocart and Harris in sanctioning use of the term "supernatural." While recognizing the convenience of the term, he holds that that convenience is existentially grounded: that what all religions have in common, and what identifies them as pertaining to a distinctive category labeled religion, is a sense of the supernatural. To quote him, "the supernatural marks the unity of all religion ... the basis of religion is the belief in the supernatural" (1983:252). Hultkrantz maintains, moreover, that certain terms used by some North American Indians can be glossed "supernatural," especially if we understand the ethnographic contexts in which those terms are used (1983:245–52).

Now, in addition to considerations that might be raised from a reading of Goodman's essay on similarity, there is a major ethnographic concern attendant on what we may call "the analogy and convenience argument" set forth by Harris, Hocart, and others. I have already raised this issue in my discussion of Hallowell, and it deserves to be discussed further.

Widespread cross-cultural applications of the term "supernatural," as Hallowell warns, would impose our cultural subjectivities on descriptions of the subjectivities of populations that may not closely approximate to them. Some may consider that a minor cost. Others, however, deem it more serious, especially when, like Hallowell, they are concerned with presenting non-Western ideas and beliefs to Euro-American audiences with as little distortion as possible in the translation process. As the sociologist W. C. Runciman (1969:150) rightly and succinctly puts it, "[a]lthough beliefs of any sort may be legitimately explained in categories foreign to the subjects themselves, they can only be identified in the subjects' own terms."

Despite such possible costs, numbers of social scientists employ the term "supernatural" cross-culturally. Most of them, however, fail to offer definitions of the term. And among those who do proffer definitions, we find an interesting assortment.

Durkheim and those either explicitly influenced by him (e.g., LévyBruhl 1936:5) or otherwise in effective agreement with him (e.g., Hallowell 1960) rule out many cross-cultural applications of the term. Durkheim, it may be recalled, ties the term to a sense of the "impossible" supported by the modern "positive sciences." And Hallowell maintains that the Northern Ojibwa lack a category of nature.

Some other social scientists cautiously offer a definition of supernatural that is explicitly based on Euro-American usages, separating the question of possible cross-cultural applications from the substance of an orienting definition. The British social anthropologist, Sir Edward E. Evans-Pritchard, gives us this example:

> We have a notion of an ordered world conforming to what we call natural laws, but some people in our society believe that mysterious things can happen which cannot be accounted for by reference to natural laws and which therefore are held to transcend them, and we call these happenings supernatural. To us supernatural means very much the same as abnormal or extraordinary.
>
> (Evans-Pritchard 1937:80)

Then there are social scientists—probably the largest number among those who define the term—who offer what they seem to suppose are universal characterizations of the supernatural. The sociologist Rodney Stark, for example, writes the following: "Supernatural refers to somewhat mysterious forces or entities that are above, beyond, or outside of nature and which may be able to influence reality" (2007:10). Stark applies this definition when he defines gods as "supernatural beings having consciousness and intentions"

(2007:10). By "somewhat mysterious," I take him to be making a realistic point: if the "forces" or "entities" referred to were entirely "mysterious," our cognitive machinery could not process them. In any case, Stark's definition of supernatural is not as stark as Durkheim's definition. Lacking Durkheim's insistence on "the impossible," it has a wider extension. Yet I do not deem Stark's formulation to be entirely satisfying.

Are we to think of the "somewhat mysterious forces or entities" to which Stark refers as metaphysical posits or as epistemological conundrums? Were it the latter, then Stark's definition might include phenomena that scientists have not (or have not yet) reconciled with their conceptualizations of nature—or, to put it differently, scientists have not yet altered their conceptions of nature to accommodate those anomalies. But inasmuch as modern scientists do not ordinarily label such phenomena "supernatural," Stark's definition would seem to apply to metaphysical posits more readily than to epistemological conundrums.

In Stark's definition supernatural entities or forces as metaphysical posits are outside of (or above or beyond) the limits of nature as someone conceives of—and apparently bounds—nature. But while such talk of nature and its limits may be acceptable to Westerners, is it not (for reasons given by Hallowell) an imposition on the cultural subjectivities of the northern Ojibwa and similar non-Western people? And if it is (as appears to be the case), is that an acceptable cost? Hallowell (1960), Klass (1995), and others argue that it is not.

The third and final cost—perhaps the most costly cost—is of a different sort. Numbers of social scientists tend to employ supernatural as a cover term for various entities and forces in which others are said to believe—others, but not the social scientist. That is, as I pointed out earlier, application of the word "supernatural" may reflect, advertently or inadvertently, a social scientist's judgment that the entities and forces to which he or she applies the term do not exist except as mistaken beliefs.

The mistaken beliefs are held to be real, but the entities or forces affirmed by them are deemed nonexistent.

In holding that the supernatural entities and forces affirmed in the beliefs of those whom they study are unreal, social scientists logically suppose that those entities and forces can have no causal significance in themselves. Beliefs about them, however, can have causal significance. One of the tasks of the social scientist is to trace out the consequences of entertaining such beliefs. And another task of the social scientist is to offer explanations of why people—other people—might affirm such beliefs.

In short, the term "supernatural" is sometimes employed to mark out entities and forces that the social scientist regards as unreal and therefore empty of causal significance in themselves—but that must nevertheless be described and explained existentially, functionally, and, if possible, historically and psychologically. The widespread use of the term "supernatural" by social scientists thus relates to genuine differences in outlook between social scientists and many whom they study. And the seemingly untroubled use of the term "supernatural" by the great majority of social scientists—untroubled to the extent of seldom being questioned and analyzed by them—in effect serves to paper over differences between social scientists and the populations about whom they write.

Such differences, I think, might be better confronted directly. I have heard ethnographers remark that while they do not endorse some of their informants' beliefs, they nevertheless "respect" those beliefs. The student of religion Robert Segal, however, raises a serious question about such "respect," both as a general matter and with particular reference to many scholars of religion:

> [Scholars] can profess to "respect" the believer's point of view. But such respect is self-deceptive. One cannot respect what one denies. One cannot will respect or grant it blindly.
>
> (Segal 1989:21)

One begins to wonder if a latent or seldom recognized function of the concept of the supernatural is the promotion of irony. Among at least some social scientists the culturally supported convictions that others display about the supernatural are deemed to be wool pulled over what otherwise might be clear-seeing eyes. But in claiming to "respect" those convictions, do not our social scientists pull a bit of wool over their own eyes? While virtually all of us find beliefs in the supernatural to be interesting and well worth studying and theorizing about, it would be closer to the truth, I think, for most of us to speak of tolerance rather than respect in the conduct of our scholarly work.

2

Nature and Transcendence among the Ancient Greeks

Social scientists with more than a passing interest in the development of one or another category of the supernatural will find much to whet their appetites as they scroll through the prolific records left to us by the ancient Greeks. We find in those records systematic efforts to characterize and to account for "nature" (*phúsis*). We also find a variety of constructs that are likely to remind us of what many of our contemporaries term "supernatural"—gods, spirits, ghosts, prodigies, monsters, oracles, and other remarkable and mysterious entities, events, and forces. We may nevertheless ask, did the ancient Greeks actually recognize a category of the supernatural? If by that question we mean, "Did the ancient Greeks explicitly conceptualize a domain of the 'supernatural' in contrast to a domain of the 'natural'?" then my answer is "no." That is so even though the ancient Greeks enjoyed a vocabulary and other intellectual resources that could endow a more or less stable distinction between the supernatural and the not-supernatural. But my "no" is entered with hesitation, a hesitation occasioned mainly by three considerations.

First, our heritage from the ancient Greeks is so rich, so diverse, and so complex that often enough existential claims or hortatory admonitions made by some Greeks find their obverse or converse in the affirmations of other Greeks. In my readings it seems that some came closer to conceptualizing what I understand by the term "supernatural" than did others.

Second, our heritage from the Greeks, though rich and complex, is nevertheless a limited heritage. It is in great measure a literary heritage, produced by members of intellectual elites. While our analyses of ancient Greek literatures, supplemented by what we know and can infer of Greek art, architecture, and material culture, tell us much about lower classes (including slaves) in ancient Greek civilization, they don't tell us all that we would like to know. In the absence of adequate data about the lower classes, we may sometimes default to, and overgeneralize about, presumptively better supported generalizations about the elites. This fact of life affects my discussion of nature and transcendence among the ancient Greeks. In reading what I write, the reader should bear it in mind that my claims really extend to some of the ancient Greeks, not to all of them.

Third, we moderns are variously biased in what we deem charming and important in ancient Greek thought, and that affects our analyses and conclusions in significant ways. Two examples—the German romantic poet Friedrich Schiller and the French historian and structuralist Jean-Pierre Vernant—may prove instructive.

In his poem, "The Gods of Greece," Schiller imagines a vibrant, meaningful, and fulfilling sense of nature in ancient Greek paganism:

> Man gifted nature with divinity
> To lift and link her to the breast of love;
> All things betrayed to the initiate eye
> The track of gods above!

When nature was so gifted, Schiller imagines, there was neither "stern self-denial" nor "sharp penance" in human life. Each heart could be happy, "[f]or the gods, the happy ones, were kin to man." But pagan enchantment did not withstand the coming of Christianity: "To enrich the worship of the one / A universe of gods must pass away." "Home to the poet's land the gods are flown," and now, Schiller laments, "Like the dead timepiece godless nature creeps."

Well, we may ask, what of the supernatural? If poetic vision posits pervasive enchantment in nature and in human life, is that likely to leave significant room for the supernatural? I think not, for if all nature be deemed enchanted, what need would there be for the supernatural?

Taking a very different tack, Jean-Pierre Vernant (1983) argues that from its early beginnings ancient Greek philosophy moved in the direction of "positivism." It did so principally by preferring rational accounts of nature to those that pivot on magic and miracles (later in this chapter I quote the classicist W. K. C. Guthrie [1967] who makes a similar point with specific reference to the Milesian philosophers). Vernant's view, I think, has much to commend it. Like many contemporary assertions about ancient Greek thought, however, it can stand a bit of tempering. For alongside of what may strike us as examples of Greek rationalism we encounter diverse landscapes of enchantment. Rationality and enchantment sometimes coexist, and on occasion they color one another. Thus, for instance, Plato's ideas about an immortal soul (to be discussed later in this chapter) are not made entirely out of philosophical cloth but appear to be woven of threads from different sources, some of them pertaining to religion and to mystical aspirations.

In considering the rich complexity of Greek thought, one way to begin an inquiry about whether or not the ancient Greeks explicitly recognized a domain of the supernatural comparable to ours is to dissect our supernatural analytically. That is, we break our concept down into constituent elements. In order to understand Greek thought, in short, we begin with our thought.

If we think analytically about our notions of the supernatural, one component or aspect is especially likely to command our attention: the idea of transcendence. For us, the supernatural is typically that which is "beyond" or "above"—and therefore deviates from or is an exception to—the normal course of nature. The ancient Greeks had ideas along those lines, even to the point of describing some human beings as "god-like." But before considering examples of transcendence in Greek thought, we would do well to pause and recognize that talk about transcendence can be tricky.

I return to the idea of transcendence later in this chapter, but here I begin with some ideas expressed by the philosopher Edith Wyschograd in *Transcendence* (1981). She notes that talk about transcendence in Euro-American societies tends to employ metaphors of spatial exteriority. The general imagery conveyed by such metaphors is that of something outside of a boundary or beyond a limit. Yet, she observes,

> [W]hatever transcends, whether conceived as unlimited in the absolute sense, or as unsurpassable by any other being, acquires its meaning by virtue of its elusiveness. For if the object has been obtained, a limit has been transgressed. What is exterior has been incorporated into a totality and what transcends now lies elsewhere.
>
> (Wyschograd 1981:59–60)

Specifying what is beyond a boundary may prove boundary transgressing, and some have used their recognition of that possibility to construct more inclusive systems. A case in point—a not especially complex one for illustrative purposes—is afforded by the efforts of Horace Bushnell, a nineteenth-century American Protestant theologian, to include nature and the supernatural in one system. He identifies the supernatural as something that escapes the causal necessities of nature. The supernatural, Bushnell (1910 [1858]:31) writes, "meets us in what is least transcendent and most familiar, even in ourselves ... The very idea of our personality is that of a being not under the law of cause and effect, a being supernatural." But having so identified to his own satisfaction the supernatural in contrast to nature, Bushnell incorporates both into a larger system. His major theological publication on the subject is entitled *Nature and the Supernatural as Together Constituting the One System of God* (1858).

During the last century or so Western philosophers and theologians have analytically distinguished, and named, several sorts of transcendence. The philosopher W. D. Hudson (1977), for instance, contrasts "logical transcendence" (which has to do with the amount of strain that a language may tolerate in expressing religious ideas before unintelligibility sets in) with "empirical transcendence" ("that overplus," Hudson writes, "of some property or properties which always seem to distinguish god from man"). And the theologian Gordon Kaufman (1972) proffers models of two kinds of transcendence, "teleological transcendence" (based on a human capacity to set goals and then organize one's life to achieve them) and "interpersonal transcendence" (based on the fact that in interpersonal relations alter is partially "transcendent" because we cannot know everything about him or her). (See Saler 2000 [1993] for discussions of these and other concepts of transcendence and their bearings on religion.)

For present purposes, however, a basic set of dictionary definitions of "transcendence" would seem to suffice: "Surpassing or excelling others of its kind; going beyond the ordinary limits; superior or supreme; extraordinary" (*Oxford English Dictionary* 253). The ancient Greeks operated with those senses of transcendence. But did that imply a category termed "supernatural"? I think not. Let us sample some relevant examples of classical Greek thought.

The Milesian Physicists

In the sixth century BCE, the city of Miletus was home to three legendary pre-Socratic Greek philosophers, Thales, Anaximander, and Anaximenes. Miletus, located on the western coast of Asia Minor (today's Turkey), was a trading center in the days of the Milesian philosophers. It was populated mainly by persons whose native language was a dialect of Greek spoken throughout Ionia, an area that included a strip of the Asia Minor mainland and a number of nearby islands in the Aegean Sea. Other residents included merchants and commercial brokers (and sometimes their families and servants). The polyglot nature of Miletus's population, and the lively sea-borne trade that sustained that population, some historians suppose, resulted in a multiculturalism that stimulated curiosity, a curiosity that eventuated, tradition has it, in a philosophical tradition that broke with parochial mythologies and that opted for secular, universalist claims on reason.

Our notions about the Milesian philosophers largely derive from authors who lived two or more centuries later than they. Aristotle, for example, wrote about them in *The Metaphysics*. And his student Theophrastus is credited with a compilation of their various alleged pronouncements (along with those of some other early philosophers). In addition to problems in deciding which textual fragments and later accounts may authentically capture the views of the Milesians, there is the related problem of understanding meanings in the fragments attributed to them. Michael Stokes (1971:64), a scholar who wrestled with that problem, maintains that "[p]ractically any statement concerning Milesian linguistic usage is based on nothing but conjecture."

Despite the difficulties and discouragements alluded to above, an intellectual portrait—indeed, an inspiring intellectual portrait—of the Milesian philosophers has been constructed. Not only that, but it has been accepted to a great extent by such eminent and diverse twentieth-century scholars as Robin G. Collingwood (1945), Werner Jaeger (1947), William K. C. Guthrie (1967), and Karl R. Popper (1972). All find something in the traditional portrait to admire, particularly when what they admire harmonizes with their own respective advocacies. Thus, for instance, the famous author of *Conjectures and Refutations: The Growth of Scientific Knowledge* (1962) and *Objective Knowledge: An Evolutionary Approach* (1972) tells us that "doubt and criticism ... become ... part of the tradition of the [Milesian] school," and in the course of critical discussions "observation is called in as a witness" (Popper 1972:348). Our contemporary knowledge claims about the Milesian philosophers remind me of a maxim that the sociologist Pitrim Sorokin translated (liberally, I suspect) into English from Russian: "When there is no fish, a crayfish is a fish." It is in the spirit of that maxim that I reproduce below some of what is claimed about the philosophical outlook and influence of the fabled Milesians.

The Milesians are credited with beginning critical philosophy in the West, and the first of their company, Thales, is sometimes hailed as "the father of philosophy." They are esteemed for developing critical attitudes toward received doctrines and myths. The Milesians, moreover, are of interest because of their speculations about *phúsis*, a term that is glossed into Latin as *natura* and into English as "nature." Aristotle and other Greeks described the Milesians as *phúsikoi*, "physicists," or *phusiólogoi*, "students" or "theorists" of *phúsis*.

Phúsis, like the terms *natura* and "nature," is polysemic. That is, it has multiple meanings, meanings that are systematically related to one another. According to F. H. Sandbach (1975:31), its basic meaning is "growth," then, by extension, "the way a thing grows" and "the way a thing acts and behaves." By a further extension it came to mean "the force that causes a thing to act and behave as it does." Werner Jaeger (1947:20) writes that *phúsis* relates to the act of *phûnai*, "the process of growth and emergence." Jaeger adds that the term also came to include the source or origin of things, "that from which they have grown, and from which their growth is constantly renewed—in other words, the reality underlying the things of our experience" (1947:20).

In our conventional contemporary portrait of the Milesian philosophers, the three leading figures, Thales, Anaximander, and Anaximenes, purportedly supposed that all of the many different things of the world arose from the existence of some original substance or ground principle (Jaeger 1947). Questions about the specifics of origin and derivation collectively frame what is known as the Problem of the One and the Many, the problem of how many different things arose from one. In the sixth century BCE, we are told that problem occupied the mutual attentions of the three great Milesian philosophers. Each, moreover, is said to have proffered different claims about the nature of the original stuff and about how it may have morphed into multiplicity. Thales identified the original unity as "water," Anaximander as something "without limits" (ápeiron) but otherwise unspecifiable, and Anaximenes as "air."

I need not supply further allegations about the respective Milesian theories. With respect to our interest in the construction of the supernatural, however, we are obliged to consider the dominant contemporary overview on the nature and thrust of Milesian philosophizing. That overview is concisely expressed by the distinguished classicist William K. C. Guthrie (1967). As Guthrie puts it, "no European" before the Milesians "had set out to satisfy his curiosity about the world in the faith that its apparent chaos concealed a permanent and intelligible order, and that the natural order could be accounted for by universal causes operating within nature itself and discoverable by human reasoning." In so attempting to account for the natural order, Guthrie goes on to write, the Milesians "consciously rejected the mythical and religious tradition of their ancestors, in particular its belief in the agency of anthropomorphic gods" (1967:441).

Assuming that that overview is correct—I personally wouldn't bet the fishing fleet on it, but for want of evidence to the contrary we perforce take it seriously—the Milesians developed a view of nature that in some respects approximated to that which Durkheim credits to the modern positive sciences (and to them alone). If so, might the supernatural have been a "conquest" of Milesian philosophy? The evidence, such as it is, gives us no reason to suppose that that was so.

Our textbook accounts of the Milesian philosophers stress their disinclination to account for the natural world by invoking anthropomorphic gods (or, by implication, other forces or entities that we might call supernatural).

We need not regard the mysterious statement attributed to Thales, "Everything is full of gods," as an exception, especially in light of the polysemy of *theós*, the usual Greek term for god. Of greater moment in our traditional portrait of the Milesians is the understanding that the emergence of the many from the one came not from a creator outside of nature but from generative powers within it. All of nature is derived from nature by natural processes, leaving no apparent role for the supernatural or for a seemingly unnatural transcendence. Instead of personalistic explanations that resemble those that Hallowell describes for the Northern Ojibwa, the Milesians apparently opted for impersonal causation, a causation devoid of the capriciousness that we and the Greeks sometimes attribute to the agency of persons.

Currents in Ancient Greek Philosophy

We can read much of ancient Greek philosophy as an intellectual struggle against the assignment of causal powers in nature to the capricious or the unpredictable or the unreasonable. Various philosophers have sometimes called on myth and the gods, but not—in most of the cases that we deem particularly memorable and worthy of attention—in order to affirm a supernatural transcendence. Rather, mythology and religion, in the literatures that we especially cherish, furnished materials that were re-worked in the service of philosophy.

Curiously enough, the archaic and classical Greeks had an adjective—*huperphuēs*—that actually did mean "supernatural" in later times. It originally meant "growing above ground," and it came to mean "overgrown," "tangled," "enormous," "monstrous," "outlandish," and so forth. It is used by the fifth century BCE pre-Socratic philosopher Democritus of Abdera in his account of why we may perceive images of the gods when we are asleep. That explanation, however, is starkly materialistic. And although Democritus allows for the existence of the gods as superhuman beings, his philosophy concedes no ground to the supernatural.

Democritus of Abdera

Some have called Democritus (c. 460–370 BCE) "the laughing philosopher" because he usually seemed to be in high good humor. Some have also called him "the father of science," not only because of his salient materialism but also because he advocated a mechanistic view of explanation (that is, he favored explanations that posit antecedent causes rather than final causes).

Democritus and his teacher Leucippus were the two leading figures of early atomism. They argued that all discernible objects in the universe are made of "atoms" (*atomos* literally means "uncuttable"—irreducible, that is, to something smaller or more basic). Atoms, in their view, are eternal (they cannot be created or destroyed), they are infinite, they differ in shape and size, they are perpetually in motion, and they relate and connect to other atoms in various ways. Since atoms are in motion, they must have empty space in which to move, to collide and connect with other atoms, and to alter their shapes. The two atomists maintained that what is fundamentally real in the universe are atoms and "the void" (empty space); everything else is "opinion."

The notion of empty space, however, was problematic among some of the ancient Greeks. In, for instance, a paradox posed by Parmenides of Elea in his argument against motion as a pivotal concept in the philosophy of nature, a void is a nothing, and how can we logically affirm the existence of a nothing? The atomists took that problem in stride, and they scored some points for early empiricism. Motion, they pointed out, is often observable, and motion requires empty space. End of problem. (For them, anyway.)

The business-like attitude displayed by the atomists is grounded in their theory of perception. All objects that exist, they held, are not only composed of atoms, but those atoms, as is the nature of atoms, progressively slough off. In doing so, they retain relations to other atoms that simultaneously emanate from the same object, forming a film of atoms. Such films tend to shrink, and in so doing they may make impressions on our eyes, thus accounting in part for what we see (the sensitivities of the eyes must also be taken into account). The sensible features of objects are thus traceable to the relational properties of atoms. Material films of atoms are the "images" (*eidola*) that we perceive.

This decidedly materialist theory applies to the gods, the gods also being composed of atoms. Democritus apparently supposed that the gods constitute a class of existents, that they dwell in upper regions of the air, and that they give off very fine films of atoms so that they are more likely to be perceived when we are relaxed in sleep than when awake. The gods, moreover, may sometimes communicate with sleeping humans and give them advice and even predictions about the future.

In the tradition passed on to us by Sextus Empiricus (Diels 1960:178, Sext. *adv. math* IX 19, Democ. B, 166), the images of the gods that people sometimes see in their sleep are "large and exceeding human stature (*huperphuē*) and hard to destroy, but not indestructible." While the Greek adjective just cited eventually came to mean, among other things, "supernatural," it would make no sense to translate it as such here. "Exceeding human stature" follows nicely after "large" and it complements Democritus's materialist theology. For Democritus, the gods cannot be creators of the world since the world is fashioned by the actions of an infinity of material entities called atoms that are eternally in motion. Nor can the gods ultimately direct or rule the world, since the nature and course of the world depend on regularities in the motions of atoms. At best (and perhaps in a bow to public opinion), Democritus seems willing to grant the gods a certain prescience and other powers. This can be taken to imply that the gods are superhuman. But superhuman in the philosophizing of the atomists is not supernatural.

Plato, the Transcendent Forms, and the Immortal Soul

Plato (*c.* 429–347 BCE) draws on myth in constructing narratives and in listening in on dialogues while extolling what he understands to be reason. In the Timaeus he even has a mythic creator of sorts, an artisangod, the Demiurge. Plato's Demiurge is an interesting construct. It orders the physical world in accordance with the Forms or Ideas, which Plato treats as real, as actually existing in a transcendent realm.

The Transcendent Forms

In his ontology of *Forms* Plato exalts the perfect over the imperfect. The formal, geometrical Idea of the Circle, for example, signals perfection in contrast to the imperfections of the usual pottery plates and other circular things that we encounter in sensate experience. Even were we to come upon a seemingly perfect circular pottery plate, that plate would only constitute a temporary and contingent instance of circularity and not circularity itself. Platonic transcendence, in extolling the perfect over the imperfect, affirms the superiority of the eternal and the immutable in contrast to the transitory and the malleable. Genuine perfection, Plato insists, implies eternal changelessness, for any change in something perfect would necessarily be a change away from perfection. While the pottery plates that our artisans make are not only likely to be imperfect in circularity to some degree or other, but when they chip or break they change, and their seeming circularity is compromised or destroyed. The Idea of the Circle, however, forever and universally remains the same.

Platonic transcendence also celebrates ratiocination over sensate experience. The Idea of the Circle is only accessible to the mind, a manifestation of the soul. It contrasts in that regard with circular-appearing things that we bring into awareness through the senses. The transcendent Forms or Ideas belong to the realm of the Intelligibles, "the things that are" (*ta onta*), whereas sensate, transitory experiences belong to the realm of the Sensibles, "the things that become" (*ta gignōmena*).

Now, the transcendent Forms or Ideas—the Intelligibles accessible only to the mind—do not combine with the Sensibles, the contingent and transitory particulars of experience that come into awareness through the senses. Rather, the Ideas or Forms exist apart by themselves (*kath auta*) (*Phaedo* 129D–130A). The relationship between Sensibles and Intelligibles is conceived to be asymmetric. That is, the Intelligibles do not depend on the Sensibles, whereas the Sensibles are dependent on the Intelligibles. The Sensibles have their being and qualities because they "participate" for some discrete time in the eternal Forms or Ideas, the Intelligibles, that share their names. Thus, for instance, when we deem a flower "beautiful," it is because it participates for some brief time in the Idea of Beauty. And although our flower will soon wither and decay, the Idea of Beauty will remain, uncompromised, immutable, and eternal.

The above is a capsule description of the most famous example of Platonic transcendence. The Forms or Ideas, the Intelligibles, are separate from the Sensibles. They transcend them. Genuine knowledge, *epistēmē*, is knowledge of the Forms or Ideas; we only have "opinions" about the Sensibles.

Philosopher I. M. Crombie, in noting that in Plato the Forms are not expository fictions but, rather "the originals of which the natures of physical things [are] images or reflections" (1962:51), goes on to render this interpretation:

> The essential clue to the status of the forms is surely the doctrine that the organization of the natural world is the work of a creative mind which is totally independent of that which it creates. Without this doctrine Platonism is totally unintelligible; with it, everything falls into place.
>
> (Crombie 1962:51–2)

Crombie and numbers of others find support for this thesis in various distinct statements made by Plato. Thus in Book X of *The Laws* Plato maintains that it is a mistake to suppose that minds evolved from the physical world. Rather, for Plato, the physical world itself owes its existence to the ordering work of mind (Crombie 1962:52). The relationship between mind—divine and human—and the physical world, however, is more complex than the foregoing assertions may suggest.

According to Plato and Aristotle, Crombie writes, the human mind is a receptive phenomenon in that its thoughts are essentially existing independently of itself. Circularity, for example, is not an idea that we form; it is an objective principle that we recognize (Crombie 1962:53). Where does such an objective principle come from? According to Crombie, Plato allows for a divine intelligence as the source, an intelligence existing independently of the physical world. Such an allowance, Crombie (1962:53) suggests, helps explain the independence of the Forms, for if you believe in a divine intelligence existing independently of the world, "then you will give to the principles comprehended by such an intelligence an equally independent status."

Now, a divine intelligence independent of the world, transcendent Forms or Ideas that exist by themselves in a realm of their own, and receptive human minds, as well as a mythic artisan-god who orders the world in accordance with the Forms—all these suggest the supernatural. They clearly do so from our perspective. But what of Plato and his fellows? Some additional data on Plato may be useful.

Plato's Concepts of the Immortal Soul

In describing and discussing the immortal soul and its afterlife Plato depicts what contemporary Euro-Americans tend to regard as supernatural objects and events. His accounts—please note the plural form of the noun!—not only reflect Orphic and Pythagorean imaginings, but they also express certain of Plato's apparently original efforts at myth-making, a myth-making that both allows for the guidance of philosophical overviews and that accords a privileged place to philosophers. Further, some of the mythic accounts rendered conflict in various particulars with others. What we read in the *Phaedo* about the reincarnation of souls, for example, is not in full accord with what we read in the *Republic*, nor does the glimpse of an afterlife supplied in the *Phaedrus* find straight-forward confirmation in the *Timaeus*. Subtle and unsubtle differences in the visions vouchsafed may trouble those of us who would like a neat and tidy world (and/or a neat and tidy other world). Plato himself, however, seems to be rather relaxed about the consistency and accuracy of his accounts. Thus, for instance, after giving one version of his views on the soul and an afterlife, he remarks that "this or something like it is true" (Something like It?) (*Phaedo* 114D). How cool can you get? Giovanni Reale, holder of the Chair in the History of Ancient Philosophy at the Catholic University of Milan, furnishes us with an excellent, succinct overview of Plato's several views on "[t]he immortality of the soul, its ultraterrestrial destiny, and its reincarnation" (1990:141–55), and I draw upon his work as well as that of some others. Before dealing substantively with some of Plato's accounts, however, I think it worthwhile to point out two things about Reale's overview.

First, Reale finds truth in Plato's myths, despite what may strike us as inconsistencies and far-out imaginings. On Reale's reading of Plato, that ancient Greek philosopher not only warns against taking myths literally, but by so advising us, and by exercising philosophical controls, he "demythologizes their fantastic elements" (Reale 1990:148). The truth of Platonic mythology, Reale maintains, is to be found in its functions as allegory and in its "value [as] an 'incantation' to allay doubts and to help one's faith" (1990:152). Here the Italian scholar's approach to myth appears to be in broad agreement with that of the French scholar Paul Veyne, whom I discuss elsewhere in this chapter.

Second, Reale draws a grand conclusion from Plato's various accounts, despite their differences. "From the *Gorgias* to the *Timaeus*," he writes, "this fundamental principle is generally firm, although there are fluctuations in the way it is presented; what gives meaning to this life is the eschatological destiny of the soul; that is, the other life here has meaning only if it is related to a hereafter" (1990:154–5).

In approaching Plato's imaginings, it is worth noting that for Plato (and, indeed, for other believers in a "soul"), soul concepts are typically extensions of concepts about the self (Hallowell 1955 [1954]). To envision a postmortem career for the soul is to envision a postmortem career for the self. That is so regardless of how much—or how little—imagined continuity there may be between pre-death and projected post-death experiences. For Plato, as we may well expect, philosophical convictions and advocacies about a worthy life find complements in his ideas about the soul and its transmigrations. In profoundly revealing ways much of Plato's philosophizing about human life is given expression and support in his various suppositions and speculations about the soul and an afterlife.

Briefly put, Plato held that the soul is immortal and that when it couples with the body it animates the body. He did not simply assert those opinions. Rather, he attempted to furnish reasoned proofs for them, as, for instance, in his discussion (*Phaedrus* 245c–246a) of the difference between what is animate (*empsuchos*) and what is inanimate (*apsuchos*) and the role of the *psuchē* (the animator, the soul).

According to Plato, the soul is not only immortal, but it is radically distinct from the body. Upon the death of the body, the liberated soul is likely to suffer a fate determined by the course of its terrestrial life. As Socrates tells Cebes (*Phaedo* 81C–82C), for instance, souls "who have chosen injustice and tyranny and robbery pass into the bodies of wolves and hawks and kites. Where else can we imagine that they go?" In the *Republic*, however, we are given a somewhat different and more complex set of ideas about what happens after death. Reward and punishment for a life lived on earth cannot be eternal, Plato held, since the number of souls is limited, and eternal reward and punishment would eventually use up the supply available for human existence on earth (Reale 1990:151). (As a Wall Street broker might say with admiration, "Plato paid attention to his numbers!") Plato maintains that after the death of the body souls undergo extraterrestrial rewards or punishments for a thousand years or, in the case of souls that have committed great crimes, two thousand years, and then they are reincarnated. The *Phaedrus* (248E–249B) adds other complexities not fully harmonious with the account in the *Republic*. As Reale (1990:153–4) summarizes it,

> After ten thousand years have passed, all souls get back their wings and return to the vicinity of the Gods. The souls that for three consecutive lives have lived according to philosophy are made an exception and enjoy a kind of privilege, in which their wings are refitted after only three thousand years. It is clear, hence, that in the Phaedrus, the place in which the souls live with the Gods (and to which they return every ten thousand years) and the place in which they enjoy their reward every thousand years for each life that they live are wholly different.

Now, in ascending to the realm of the gods souls renew their original familiarity with the Forms or Ideas. The realm of the Forms is the true home of both gods and souls. But in consequence of the traumas of reincarnation, as commonly observed in the rigors of the birth-process, souls suffer amnesia. Most importantly, they lose memory of the Forms. Souls that transmigrate to humans, however, may recover at least part of that memory through skillful philosophizing. Indeed, Plato's Socrates suggests that the really good philosopher is something of a therapist.

Through skillful questioning and prodding, the philosopher helps cure the amnesia of his fellow humans. He thus assists in at least a partial recovery of the only genuine knowledge (*epistēmē*) possible for humans, knowledge of the

Forms and their relation to the organizing Form of the Good. That, basically, is the "Socratic Method," as understood by Socrates and Plato. In contrast to the vagaries that some of our contemporary educators proffer under the label of "the Socratic Method," its Greek originators deemed it a way for restoring to consciousness what the student—we might say patient—already knows in consequence of the nature and experiences of his soul.

Now, what about the soul and the supernatural? Many of Plato's multiple ideas about the soul are examples of what we call the supernatural. As Reale puts it, "Plato' s philosophy was impregnated through and through with a strongly religious sentiment" (Reale 1990:139). That is, with the hallmarks of religion. In that "[t]he soul is the intelligible and immaterial aspect of man, and it is eternal as the intelligible and immaterial is eternal" (Reale 1990:140). Plato's efforts to offer philosophical proofs or arguments respecting the soul end in what Reale (1990:140) describes as "a mediation between the rationalistic position of Socrates, on the one hand, and the mystic view of Orphism, on the other." Plato's postulation of the soul's capacity to know immutable and eternal entities, Reale (1990:141) points out, depends on a necessary condition. That is, in order to know immutable and eternal entities such as the Forms, the soul, Plato argues, must have

> a nature akin to them: otherwise these entities will remain outside its capacity; and therefore as these are immutable and eternal, so also the soul must be immutable and eternal ... (And ... when the soul and body are together, the soul governs and leads; whereas the body obeys and is led by the soul; but it is characteristic of the divine to command and of the mortal to be commanded; hence the soul—also from this viewpoint—is akin to the divine, whereas the body is akin to the mortal). As a result of a divine decree souls are not subject to death just as all things directly produced by the Demiurge are not subject to death.
>
> (Reale 1990:145)

Plato's human soul, in summary, is divinely generated and is itself divine. It belongs to the realm of the transcendent Forms, but its existences in that realm are interrupted by rebirths in bodily form. When joined with the human body, the soul directs that corruptible and transitory phenomenon while it is simultaneously imprisoned by it. And just as the body pertains to visible, sensible reality, so does the soul pertain to invisible, intelligible reality.

To summarize in more analytical terms much of what has been described in earlier pages, Plato conceptualizes reality in terms of multi-element structural oppositions. On one side of a strongly marked binary divide he posits the unchanging, the eternal, the intelligible, the invisible, the soul, and genuine knowledge (*epistēmē*). On the other side he affirms the mutable, the transitory, the sensible, the visible, the body, and contingent opinion (*doxa*). And he deems the first set superior to the second. He supposes, moreover, that the members of each set stand in a necessary relation to the other members of their set. Further, while we humans are illustrative of the second set, we are not entirely so, for we enjoy limited participations in the first. We are ensouled, Plato holds, and the sensibles of our experience, *ta gignōmena*, the things that become, are comprehensible and functional because they participate, if only briefly, in the intelligibles, *ta onta*, the things that are.

The two halves of Plato's structuralist opposition are distinguished from each other, and the first set may be said to transcend the other. But the transcendence is structural as well as metaphysical. Edith Wyschograd (1981), it may be recalled, points out in general terms that when a boundary is transgressed what was formerly transcendent is now incorporated, along with what it once transcended, into a new totality, and what may be transcendent must henceforth be sought elsewhere.

Plato indicates that the boundary between his two sets of opposed elements is in effect transgressed by the soul. But we may deem that transgression of boundaries to effect a joining of the two sets, the elements hitherto seen in analytical opposition now perceived to constitute a totalizing perspective, one that does not seem to inspire a new search for transcendence elsewhere.

Aristotle and the Unmoved Mover

Elements in the Aristotelian corpus, without themselves signaling a category of the supernatural, nevertheless play roles in the development of a Christian theology of the supernatural through their influence on Thomas Aquinas and others. Here, however, I focus on the Unmoved Mover. Aristotle calls it *theós*, "god," and he characterizes it as unchangeable, eternal, perfect, and the ultimate cause of movement in the universe. But is it supernatural as we understand that concept? Indeed, can one argue that it is "natural" in the sense of being logically entailed in Aristotle's theory of nature?

As Frederick Woodbridge (1965:55) points out, Aristotle's theory of nature is fundamentally a theory of motion. (Aristotle's teacher, Plato, also attaches great importance to motion and to a distinction between self-movement and its lack—see, for instance, *Phaedrus* 245C–246A.) While Aristotle gives somewhat different characterizations of nature in the writings attributed to him, his most famous passage regarding nature is probably this one:

> [N]ature in the primary and strict sense is the essence of things which have in themselves, as such, a source of movement; for the matter is called the nature because it is qualified to receive this, and processes of becoming and growing are called nature because they are movements proceeding from this. And nature in this sense is the source of the movement of natural objects, being present in them somehow, either potentially or in complete reality.
>
> (*The Metaphysics*, Book Lambda 1015a)

"Nature" (*phúsis*) in Aristotle's sense contrasts with "art" (*technē*), the latter lacking a source of movement in itself, either in actuality or in potentiality. It also contrasts with the creation and imposition of human "convention" or "law" (*nómos*). Those were the contrast sets that interested Aristotle, not a contrast between the natural and the supernatural.

In the *Physics* (257b) we read that "it is impossible that that which moves itself should in its entirety move itself." While movable things, according to Aristotle, have within themselves "the source of motion, not of moving something or of causing motion, but of suffering it" (*Physics* 255b), they are set in motion by something else. Setting in motion need not consist of a push or a shove. It can be inspirational, in the sense of admiring or loving and striving to emulate that which inspires to motion. And so it is for the universe. As one ascends to greater and greater degrees of perfection in the order of nature, love or admiration for the superiority of the superior inspires the inferior to movement. But unless contained this would mean infinite regress—an unending chain of movers inspiring movement—and infinite regress is intolerable to Aristotle (as it is to many other philosophers).

Aristotle wants to account for all motion in the universe, including potentiality becoming actuality, and to do so by avoiding the untidy lack of closure that we call infinite regress. He attempts to do so by postulating a mover that is outside of the natural order, the order of things that actually or potentially move. That outsider inspires movement but is itself unmoved. Logic, moreover, requires that such a mover be eternal and uncreated. That is because a non-eternal, created mover would be one that came into existence, and a coming into existence, itself an act of motion, would require an explanation. One would have to posit a cause for the motion of a non-eternal mover, and that would bring infinite regress back into the picture rather than banish it.

Aristotle's Unmoved Mover, aka *theós* ("god"), is the ultimate cause of all movement. It is immaterial, uncreated, immutable, and eternal. It is, as the

Jewish sage Maimonides pointed out, an intellectual principle in a theory of causality (Wolfson 1941:152).

The world, according to Aristotle, is uncreated and eternal, and god is not its designer. Nor does god, the Unmoved Mover, take any notice of human beings. It not only lacks what Pascal Boyer (2001:150–55) calls "strategic information" about humans, but it lacks any information at all about human beings. That is because it thinks only of its own perfection, for to think of anything else—all other things being less perfect—would be to degrade or subvert its perfection. It is "mind minding itself," and its thinking is "a thinking on thinking." It has no free will, no plans, no aspirations, no concerns as we understand concerns. It is not what we call an intentional agent. Yet it is the ultimate source of regularity and purposive action in nature. That is because imperfect nature strives to imitate its perfection.

The Poets' Gods

Aristotle's god is decidedly abstract. Aristotle's terminology, however, makes use of the remarkably rich polysemy of the Greek word *theós*. The classicist Ulrich von Wilamowitz-Möllendorff (1956 [1931]) calls our attention to the use of *theós* as a predicate term among the ancient Greeks, a usage that suggests these questions: What did the Greeks say is a god? How far did they extend the term *theós*? Where were the limits, metaphorical and otherwise, in propriety as well as in meaning? While the philosophers provide us with some data for constructing answers, the questions themselves lead us to Greek religion as well as to Greek philosophy, and that obliges us to explore the writings of the poets. As the classicist Walter Burkert (1985 [1977]:4) notes, "[t]he most important evidence for Greek religion remains the literary evidence," and that evidence includes "practically the whole of ancient poetry." Burkert adds that "religious texts in the narrow sense of sacred texts are scarcely to be found" among the ancient Greeks (1985 [1977]:4).

The poet Euripides (*Helen* 560) writes, "For recognizing friends is also a god" (theós gar kai to gignōskein philous). That statement, in all probability, was both meaningful and pleasing to his Greek audiences. It encapsulates a moral observation in an existential assertion. "God," here, makes the case that that to which it is applied, the recognizing of friends, is not only a virtue in the conduct of human life but that it is eternally so.

Anthropomorphic gods—Zeus, Athena, and so on—are often collectively referred to as *hoi athanatoi*, "the deathless ones." The gods are immortal whereas human beings are not. Further, the gods are ageless. The dreadful consequence of failing to couple deathlessness with agelessness is well illustrated by the sad story of Tithonus (*Homeric Hymn* 5: 218–38). Zeus endowed that poor fellow with immortality but not eternal youth. Over the years Tithonus progressively lost vigor, but he could not obtain relief in death. His former lover, the goddess Eos, eventually locked him away in a room where, we are told, "he babbles endlessly."

In light of the high valuation of immortality and agelessness, the extension of the term "god" from immortal and ageless sentient beings to enduring and perpetually fresh abstract principles is comprehensible and informative. It is an arresting convention for affirming the continuing value of such principles in the conduct of human life. Just as Plato and Aristotle supposed that that which is unchangeable and eternal is superior to that which is transitory and contingent, so, too, did the Greek poets celebrate—and apotheosize—timeless virtues.

In addition to being credited with immortality and agelessness, the anthropomorphic gods are also often described as collectively exceeding humans in powers and other attributes. They may, for instance, become invisible. But while individual gods typically surpass most of us in some quality or attribute, such as strength, beauty, or wisdom, the poets represent some mortals as being the equal of the gods in certain ways—even in some cases surpassing some immortals in discrete attributes. Thus, as the classicist

Erland Ehnmark (1935:3) points out with respect to the Homeric poems, while nobody is more beautiful than Aphrodite or wiser than Athena, "Achilles is undoubtedly superior to Hephaestus in physical qualities and Odysseus is more cunning than Ares."

The striking qualities of some mortals are sometimes spoken of as gifts of the gods, and the possessors of those qualities are described as godlike. Furthermore, the gods may episodically invest mortals with superlative features or qualities, such as epic courage and ardor, incredible strength, or a wondrously fearsome appearance in battle. Ehnmark concludes that

> the expression "godlike" can be something more than a mere metaphor. We are here concerned with the actual elevation of a man to a level where he becomes the equal of the gods. Man receives a share of divine power and accordingly of the divine itself. He can never achieve equality with the gods through his own unaided efforts. It is only when man's own strength is reinforced by divine power that he attains to something like divine rank. Since this power proceeds from the gods and is not inherent in man as such, the superiority in man, which makes him godlike, is not a part of his human equipment, but is a divine quality.
>
> (Ehnmark 1935:9)

Ehnmark's analysis of "godlike" in the attainment of a remarkable approximation to divine rank supports the German poet Goethe's opinion that

> [t]he purpose and goal of the Greek is to deify man, not to humanize divinity. This is not anthropomorphism but theomorphism.
>
> (Myron's Kuh, quoted in Otto 1979:236)

It also provides us with some interesting perspectives on Christianity (e.g., the claim that the Word of God "became man so that we might become God," the subtly controversial idea that grace is "superadded" to man's created nature, and the teaching that salvation, signaled by immortality and freedom from corruption and suffering, can come only from god). Here, however, I want to begin considering what may be involved in describing anthropomorphic Greek gods and theomorphized mortal heroes as "superhuman." This is a topic that I return to later. It may prove useful, however, to begin thinking about it now.

Superhuman Agents

The anthropologist Melford E. Spiro writes:

> For me, ... any definition of "religion" which does not include, as a key variable, the belief in superhuman—I won't muddy metaphysical waters with "supernatural"—beings who have power to help or harm man is counter-intuitive.
>
> (Spiro 1966:91)

Spiro goes on to define religion as "an institution consisting of culturally patterned interaction with culturally postulated superhuman beings" (1966: 96). William Scott Green, who accepts Spiro's definition, explicates "superhuman being" as "a being more powerful than humans but not necessarily qualitatively different from them. Superhuman is not the same as supernatural" (2006:7).

While Spiro was not the first to describe the gods (and, by extension, other posited spiritual beings) as superhuman, he was influential in popularizing the use of that expression in the academic study of religion. Applying the term "superhuman" is not free of problems, but the "metaphysical waters" do seem less "muddy" than in the case of applying the term "supernatural." Supernatural in popular parlance suggests an ontological classification codable in digital form. The supernatural (code it 1) contrasts with the natural (code it 0). Superhuman, in contrast, suggests an analog scale—gradual variations in degrees of human capacities and capabilities beyond what is normally the case, but progressive extensions rather than sharp breaks. Conceptualizing superhuman beings, moreover, is likely to require lesser cognitive investments in counterintuitivity than in the case of imagining supernatural beings. Here, however, with specific reference to the ancient Greeks, I enter my opinion that "superhuman" is a less problematical term than "supernatural" for describing anthropomorphized gods and theomorphized humans. Consider how some classical Greek texts attempt to account for the existence and nature of the gods.

The Origins of the Anthropomorphic Gods

There are a variety of ancient Greek sources that say something about the origins of the anthropomorphic gods. In attempting to sort them out analytically, I assign some to a group that I label "Myth" and others to a group that I label "Rationalizing Legends." The members of each group are differentially linked by family resemblances. It is probably the case, moreover, that numbers of Greeks found some accounts in each group to be more persuasive than others.

Myths

The most famous pan-Hellenic store of myths regarding the origins of the gods is Hesiod's *Theogony*. Hesiod's exact dates are unknown, but it is reasonable to guess that he lived around 700 BCE. It is probably the case that his accounts of the origins of the gods are based on older myths that circulated in his and in earlier times.

Hesiod's *Theogony* begins with the cosmos-engendering congress of "Chaos" and "wide-bosomed Earth," from which other named cosmogenic forces and beings derive. Much of the *Theogony* is given over to the genealogies and struggles of the gods of Greek religion. Zeus, king of the Olympians, for instance, is said to have overthrown the Titan Cronus, who had earlier vanquished and castrated his own father, Uranus. There is a good deal of sex and violence in the histories of the gods, but those aspects of the narratives are overwhelmed—for me, at least—by the fantastic (the highly counterintuitive) details of how the gods came to be. I cannot but wonder what the ancient Greeks made of this.

An attempt to explore issues relating to how the Greeks may have viewed many of their myths is found in a short but difficult book by Paul Veyne entitled *Did the Greeks Believe in Their Myths: An Essay on the Constitutive Imagination*. That work was first published in French in 1983 and then published in an English translation in 1988. Veyne does not give us a clear-cut yes-or-no answer to the question posed in the book's title. Rather, the complex and subtle arguments that he makes raise a number of larger issues that, in Veyne's view, need to be confronted. What do we, or what should we, mean by "belief"? What do we, or what should we, mean by "true" and "truth"?

Some indication of where Veyne appears to be going can be gleaned from statements such as these: "Men do not find the truth; they create it as they create their history" (1988: xii); a myth can be viewed as "a truth that has been altered by popular naïveté" (1988: 14); at a myth's authentic core are "small true details" (1988:14). These and similar affirmations suggest a certain truthfulness in myth. But it is not the truthfulness of the seemingly "literal" content of myth that should excite our attention. Rather, Veyne suggests, we should appreciate myths as creative acts of the imagination and as the setting forth of a special kind of reality, a constructed reality that may be accepted without overturning our commitments to workaday realities.

Now, what about the supernatural? Do the myths implicate some concept of the supernatural? In addressing that question, I begin not with Paul Veyne but with his translator, Paula Wissing. In the 1988 English translation published by the University of Chicago Press there is a Translator's Note on page ix that reads in part:

Also, I have occasionally used the somewhat gothic-sounding term "supernatural" as a gloss to the French *merveilleux* or *le merveilleux*. Although supernatural is perhaps not the best term to associate with Greek attitudes toward mythology, the context of the author's discussions sometimes makes the other less surprising terms ("marvelous," "fabulous,") confusing. The author also uses the term supernatural—rarely, to be sure, but again to refer to the realm of myth and legend as opposed to everyday reality. I hope that the more frequent use of the term does not distort his thought.

In short, for Wissing, the translator of Veyne, and no doubt for many other modern Euro-Americans, supernatural is a convenient way of calling attention to departures from "everyday reality" that are stronger, more arresting or attention-getting than would be the case were we to use words such as "marvelous" and "fabulous."

Rationalizing Legends

The presence of the supernatural is even more apparent in rationalizing legends about the origins of the gods. Perhaps the most famous of such legends derives from Euhemerus, a Sicilian Greek who lived about 300 BCE. Euhemerus's book, *The Sacred Record*, is lost. But versions of what it may have contained have been handed down to us by both Greek and Latin authors, Christians as well as pagans. The mainstream version is this: On a voyage through the Red Sea and around the coast of Arabia, Euhemerus became shipwrecked on Panchaea, an island not found in our nautical charts. On that island he came upon a temple dedicated to Zeus, and inside the temple he saw a golden pillar on which were inscribed the genealogies of various Greek gods and some other information. The inscriptions revealed that the gods had originated as exceptional mortal men and women. Their impressive deeds and benefactions had so impressed and gratified other humans that the latter elevated them to the status of gods. The import of Euhemerus's legendary discovery is not only that the gods are apotheosized human beings, but also that popular myths about the gods are often based upon real historical events, events subsequently obscured by fanciful and often fantastic narrative additions. The tenet that we may uncover historical fact in myth by boiling off exaggeration is known as "Euhemerism."

Euhemerus was neither the first nor the only Greek to maintain that the gods were originally human beings. Hecataeus of Teos, born before Euhemerus, is credited with opining that the gods of Egypt are deified benefactors of the Egyptians. And Prodicus of Ceos, a contemporary of Socrates, and Persaeus, who was mentored by Zeno the Stoic, suggested that people who discover new crops in their wanderings may be honored as gods in gratitude for the benefits that follow from their discoveries.

Indeed, cultural understandings that apotheosis is an honor to be conferred on benefactors had considerable antiquity among the Greeks. Thus, for example, in the *Odyssey* (VIII:464–8), Odysseus promises Nausicaa that when he reaches home he will honor her as he would honor a god because she had saved his life.

Superhuman

Various human characters in the Homeric poems display what we regard as superhuman qualities. The poet overtly and repetitively reminds his Greek audiences that certain mortals are impressively superior to the rank and file of humanity. Homer speaks, for example, of "godlike Alexander" (a.k.a Paris) (*Illiad* III: 17–58), he proclaims that Odysseus and Hector are "the peer of Zeus" in artifice or counsel (*Iliad* II:169), and he describes the bard Demodocus as "like the gods in speech" (*Odyssey* IX:48). Furthermore, his description of mortals who are temporarily transformed by gods into gods in appearances or functions renders those transformed mortals episodically superhuman.

And, of course, lest we forget, the gods themselves are anthropomorphically superhuman. Being superhuman, moreover, counts for quite a lot, and it explains much, in the Homeric poems and in other literary works. But so, too, does being supernatural.

And the Greek gods are certainly supernatural. That is, they are supernatural when thought of by numbers of ancient Greeks because they are at the least minimally counterintuitive in certain features (such as, for instance, being immortal). But they may not be thought of as counterintuitive when thought of by many contemporary Euro-Americans who do not actually believe in the existence of the gods. In short, for the ancient Greeks the gods were part of what we think of as nature. For us they are fictional characters; for the Greeks they were something more.

3

Some Theological Perspectives

Theology and Theologians: Some Introductory Remarks

Just as war is too important to be left to the generals, so, too, is the study of theology too important to be left to the theologians. I say this not because I think that theology provides us with important insights into the reality of the divine. Rather, the study of theology is likely to provide us with interesting insights into the reality of the human mind. In particular, studying the outputs of theologians can enhance our understandings of how intellectual elites attempt to make reflective sense of religion.

Theology typically locks on to salient elements in local religions. Not all religions, however, are supplemented by systematically thought-out and cumulative theological interpretations. Systematic theology (as distinguished from episodic and evanescent theistic speculations) depends on various continuing social supports such as guilds or priesthoods of some kind, and they in turn require social, economic, and political supports of their own. The development of agriculture ten or twelve thousand years ago helped prepare the way for the emergence and furtherance of theological specialists, as did the invention of writing about five thousand years ago. In today's world we have diverse theologies not only relating to the so-called Abrahamic religions but to others as well. But there are also numbers of contemporary religions with little or nothing in the way of disciplined and cumulative ratiocinations of the sort that I call systematic theology.

Theología/Theology

Among classical and later Greek intellectuals the term *theología* applies to a broadly figured conception of what we often call "metaphysics." Ancient Greek metaphysical conceptions usually rest on ideas about a first principle of being. Such a principle is often referred to as *theós*, a term that we may gloss as "god." In, for example, Plotinus's *Enneads*, a Neoplatonist work of the third century of the Common Era, the first principle of being is referred to both as "god" and as "The One." While Plotinus holds that The One (*to hen*) cannot be described in ordinary language—even existence cannot be predicated of it—the intellect's intuition of its metaphysical significance is required for the explanation of everything else, for all things ultimately emanate from it.

In a narrower frame of reference, we can break *theología* down into "study," "reasoning," "discourse," or "theorizing" about "*theós*." While the *theós* component of *theología* sometimes does approximate to what numbers of contemporary Euro-Americans call "god," *theós* has wider extensions among classical and later Greeks. It is sometimes a predicate term, raising the interesting question of what, in Greek usage, is a god (Wilamowitz 1956 [1931]). Classical Greek and the Greek of late antiquity are not only more expansive in what they included under the term "*theós*" than modern English is in its applications of the term "god," but the Greeks were remarkably productive in constructing divine or spiritual entities. In some later philosophies and theologies expressed in

Greek—the Neoplatonisms of Iamblichus and Proclus, for example—numbers of posited theological entities are called *theoí* ("gods") and are conceptualized in part by being arranged into ontological and functional hierarchies.

In contemporary Western Europe and the Americas, theology is often conceived to be the academically credentialed study of god or "the divine." In the course of their studies and theorizing, however, many West European and American theologians continue to deal with metaphysical questions reminiscent of what Greek intellectuals of classical and late antiquity include in the purview of the term "*theología*." It should be noted, moreover, that some contemporary members of Eastern Orthodox Churches support a somewhat different tradition respecting uses of the term "theology." "Theology" for many of them is based in significant measure on revelation and mystical experience. Numbers of Eastern Orthodox theologians are "credentialed," in a manner of speaking, by their personal religious goals and their pursuit of them in addition to, or in place of, formal academic training, in keeping with the maxim that "no one who does not follow the path of union with God can be a theologian" (Lossky 2002:39).

In sum, our term "theology" and its not-entirely-equivalent antique and present-day Greek counterparts embrace the positing of, and reasoning about, a rich diversity of constructs. Those constructs prominently include, but are not limited to, what many contemporary Euro-Americans call "god" or "gods."

Religion, Theology, and Science

In a comparison of religion and science emergent from an accumulating literature in the cognitive science of religion, Robert N. McCauley (2011) argues that in some cultures, and in certain respects, theology resembles science more than it resembles religion. In their quests for consistency and coherence, for instance, Christian theologians are likely to opt for some of the conceptual tools honored in science: systematic analysis, high-level abstraction, esoteric ideation, and deductive reasoning.

At the same time, however, the similarities between science and theology are offset by similarities between religion and theology. A salient characteristic encountered in both theology and religion is the importance that their practitioners often attach to citing some authority for their texts and/or oral traditions. Thus, for instance, Neoplatonists of late classical antiquity accord exegetical honors to Platonic texts; certain twentieth-century Roman Catholic theologians concerned with the theology of the supernatural depend on their respective exegeses of arguments advanced by Thomas Aquinas; and religious persons sometimes attempt to validate their myths by citing respected sources for them in the form of culture heroes or ancestors. In contrast, contemporary scientists are less likely to accord high value to comparable appeals to authority.

Science, theology, and religion all invent counterintuitive representations. As McCauley points out, however, while science has increasingly restricted the domains in which appeals to agent causality are credited with legitimacy, religion and theology are not only given to affirming representations of agents (gods, spirits, ghosts, etc.), but they also seek to discern the states of mind of such agents. In that respect, of course, theology is closer to religion than to science, albeit, McCauley notes, the existence of religion does not depend on theological institutions any more than it depends on literacy. Science, however, does depend on literacy, as does most systematized or formalized theologies. Furthermore, while religious representations are usually minimally counterintuitive (Boyer 1994, 2001)—the gods, for instance, are typically like human persons in most respects, their "attention-getting" counterintuitive features being few in number—both science and theology sometimes proffer radically counterintuitive claims and constructs (e.g., quantum mechanics and the doctrine of the Trinity).

In keeping with the findings and arguments of others (e.g., Barrett 1999; Boyer 2001; Slone 2004), McCauley notes that the radical counterintuitivity of theologians may not be appropriated or imitated by the rank and file of their co-religionists. That is, many of the latter harbor views that are "theologically incorrect" when compared to the pronouncements of the former. The rank and file often exhibit predilections to hold to cognitively habitual and minimally counterintuitive representations, eschewing out of ignorance and/or natural proclivities the radicalisms of theological orthodoxies. Thus, for instance, while Christian theologians may claim that their god is not only omniscient and omnipotent but also omnipresent, experimental studies accomplished by Barrett and others indicate that when ordinary Christians are asked to recall theologically correct stories about the Christian god told to them by experimenters, the divinity in their accounts is usually reported to go from one place to another, one place at a time, as is normally—and naturally—the case for human persons.

Theology often makes efforts to render religion more intelligible than it might otherwise be, just as religions typically make efforts to render our behavioral environments, our moral canons, and our coping strategies more intelligible than they might otherwise be. Religion has functioned to justify, however partially and incoherently, the activation of innate human dispositions. With the development of supportive environments theology eventually emerged in some places as systematic efforts by some intellectual elites to enlarge and render more coherent the ontologies and pragmatics of religion.

It should be noted in these introductory remarks that the term "theology" is by itself incomplete in what it designates. That is, most intellectually arresting theologies are concerned with more than god or the gods or first principles. Most of the theological systems that have come down to us include efforts to achieve coherent and relevant anthropologies. In brief, anthropology is often included in what we call theology. There are at least two reasons for that. First, comparing and contrasting god(s) and humans often amounts to a strategy for crystalizing and mapping what theologians suppose about the natures of each. Second, to the extent that theologians suppose that god or the gods make significant differences in human life, theological inferences and speculations about the gods may translate, *mutatis mutandis*, into anthropological inferences and speculations about human beings.

Cognizance of the likely anthropological implications of a serious theology may act as a constraint on theological speculations. Christian theologians, for example, in addition to being adverse to propounding theologies that overtly contradict or dismiss scriptures (the Old and New Testaments) are hesitant about propounding theologies that might seem to choke off the possibility of human salvation. While some Christian theologians, to be sure, profess to believe in salvation for only a relatively small number of "saints" (with the rest of humankind condemned to an eternity without god), few (if any) appear to insist on damnation for everyone.

In addition to theological constraints likely to stem from endorsing religious ideas about scriptures and salvation, there are others that act as brakes on theological speculations. One of the most important in Euro-American theologies is a disinclination to adopt a theology that appears to cast shadows on god's sovereignty. Anything that might seem to suggest, however inadvertently, that god is exogenously compelled, even in the service of attractive ends, is something that numbers of Euro-American theologians make efforts to avoid. Thus, for instance, numbers of theologians support Pius X's denunciation of "the old error by which a sort of right to the supernatural was claimed for human nature" (*Encyclical Pascendi Gregis* September 8, 1907). Appearing to advance such a claim is likely to excite adverse criticism among specialists concerned with the theology of the supernatural. Can theology, however, avoid seeming to limit or constrain god? Possibly, I think, but with difficulty.

Some of the reasons for difficulties pivot on similarities between science and theology that were noted by Robert McCauley (2011). To rehearse them here in somewhat more ample language, there are the self-conscious efforts of both scientists and theologians to produce consistent and coherent expositions. Both scientists and theologians mutually appreciate logical arguments. They tend to value high-level abstractions and esoteric ideations, and their assertions of relatively radical counterintuitive concepts often contrast to the minimally counterintuitive beliefs typically encountered in religions. In a manner of speaking, theologians apply science-like approaches to religious myths in order to produce better—more extended, more intelligible, and more seemingly reliable—theological myths.

The anthropological components in theology typically touch on cosmogenic and cosmological ideations that serve in some degree to situate humankind within a larger constructed reality. In Euro-American traditions this has usually involved claims about "nature" and about what may be "natural." The writings of Christian theologians are notably replete with expressions such as "nature," "nature in its entirety," "human nature," "state of pure nature," "beyond or above nature," "nature's god," "natural person," "natural desire," "natural law," "natural fulfillment," "natural end," and so forth. Despite, however, a multiplicity of different views and insights respecting nature and the natural, we can arguably discern in Christian theological treatises two major currents of meaning for those terms. One encompasses a variety of expressions that relate to the idea of nature as god's creation. The other, which does not contrast with the first but constitutes an emphasis within it, is applied specifically to human beings by Augustine of Hippo and others: nature as the state in which humans are born (what some call their "natural state").

Some figurations of what we call nature have played roles in shaping two understandings in Euro-American cultures that eventually came to be attached to the Greek adjective "supernatural" (*huperphuēs*) and to related Greek and Latin expressions of various grammatical sorts (e.g., *hupèr phúsin*, *supra naturam excedens*, *supernaturalis*). The popular understanding is that instantiations of the supernatural are remarkably unusual or mysterious when compared to instantiations of the natural order. The theological understanding rephrases in theological or "technical" language the popular understanding, and in doing so it renders the category supernatural a key factor in a soteriological theory.

Apposite to the above introductory remarks about theology and theologians, the rest of this chapter explores some examples of religion and certain related theological and philosophical claims that bear directly or indirectly on the construction of the supernatural. I start with accounts of creation given in the Hebrew Bible, accounts that became bedrock for numbers of later Christian theologies.

The Hebrew Bible and Creation

Contemporary studies of the Hebrew Bible undertaken by academics offer interpretations alternative to those usually endorsed in mainstream Judaisms and Christianities. That is especially the case with regard to the origins of the Hebrews and the origins of Israelite monotheism. Popular accounts of Hebrew origins usually repeat biblical narratives of servitude in Egypt, an exodus led by Moses, and the subsequent invasion and conquest of Canaan. Some contemporary academic scholars, in contrast, suspect that the Hebrews themselves were Canaanites and that their conquests were largely from the inside out rather than from the outside in. Instead, moreover, of simply endorsing biblical accounts of a lineal Abrahamic monotheism (albeit one that was subverted now and then by the allures of polytheism), some present-day scholars suggest that Israelite monotheism evolved in fits and starts over several centuries and that competition and syncretism relating to variously conceptualized gods (especially *El, Baal,* and *Yahweh*) reflected a complexity of economic, sociopolitical, and cultural rivalries and developments. As the biblical scholar Robert Gnuse puts it,

> One increasingly finds authors observing that in the future we ought to stress the continuity that Israelite religion had with Canaanite culture ... Serious scholars now declare that we must critically reassess our definition of monotheism in Israel and how we should speak of its emergence both in theory and our historical surveys.
>
> (Gnuse 1994:900)

Contemporary biblical scholarship in the academy is impressive. It draws upon a variety of evidential sources: philological studies and content analyses of ancient Middle Eastern texts in several languages that compare in interesting ways to biblical texts, an increasing wealth of archeological data, close readings of the Hebrew Bible that appreciate it as a literary work and that draw upon competing theories of literary criticism for illumination, and still other sources of information (including some DNA studies undertaken in efforts to establish linkages among certain human populations). Overall, contemporary academic scholarship emphasizes the Hebrew Bible as revelatory of partisan historiography in its claims to be historical. Critical emphasis in the academy is on the Hebrew Bible as an important source—in combination with other sources—for tracing cultural developments rather than as a storehouse of theological and historical truths. As it happens, some of the individuals involved in that scholarship are personally religious, and they tend to value the Hebrew Bible as an inspiring account of a people's evolving relationships with the divine. Insofar as I am aware, however, the most influential of those scholars align their personal religious commitments and their scholarly work in ways that usually allow them to function successfully in the secular academy.

In any case, individuals who contributed to the development of the theological category supernatural in the first several centuries of the Common Era contrast sharply to some (but not all) contemporary academicians. They were not critical scholars of the Hebrew Bible. Nor did they bracket or sublimate their personal theological concerns and commitments. Those who were Jews or Christians professed to regard the Hebrew Bible as a repository of truths about the creation of the world and the intervention of the divine in human history.

In Genesis 1 god creates the heavens and the earth and the created things that they contain. God initiates the creative process with a series of verbal fiats (e.g., "let there be light," "let there be an expanse in the midst of the water"). This narrative is of remarkable grandeur, and its depiction of the creator is less anthropomorphic than in the following narrative where god walks in the garden and enjoys the cool of the evening. Genesis 1 declares that prior to creation the earth was "without form and void." What existed (if that is an acceptable way of putting it) was primordial chaos, a chaos signaled by the amorphous presence of water over which hovered the wind or breath of god.

Much has been written about the biblical accounts of creation, but for my purposes I call attention to the following.

The Uncreatedness of the Biblical Creator

The creator described in the Hebrew Bible is not derived from a preexisting reality (Kaufman 1960 [1937–56]). He has no antecedent. Unlike the gods portrayed by Hesiod and other Greek writers, the god of Hebrew scriptures has no genealogy.

Creation *ex nihilo*

The biblical accounts of creation, as interpreted by numbers of believing Jews and Christians, affirm creation *ex nihilo*, creation out of nothing. Such creation is miraculous. When thought about critically within a larger— and a later—context of meanings, it implies the supernatural. The Hebrew

Bible itself does not actually term creation "miraculous" or "supernatural." But Euro-American philosophers and theologians of later times held that creation out of nothing cannot naturally occur, thus providing grounds for concluding that creation as described in the Hebrew scriptures is miraculous.

As later Jewish and Christian intellectuals note, the idea of an *ex nihilo* creation of the universe contrasts with the most famous mythical and philosophical tenets of the ancient Greeks. Classical Greek philosophers, for example, generally suppose that the world was formed or ordered out of preexistent matter. Plato takes that tack in the *Timaeus*. (Aristotle, however, maintains that the world always existed and that its structure is a necessary ordering.) But most Jewish and Christian commentators who accept the biblical account hold that their god is creator in the fullest sense—not simply (and metaphorically) an architect or a potter or some other kind of craftsman who works with what is available or a creator who creates only part of the universe, but a creator who "made everything from nothing" (as the Fourth Lateran Council puts it).

There were, to be sure, some interpreters of the Bible in the early centuries of the Common Era who favored the idea that god shaped preexistent matter or that the devil or the lesser of two posited gods made the physical world either out of preexistent matter or out of nothing, but they were not mainstream in either Judaism or Christianity.

Nature as Derivative

The biblical claim that god created the universe is generally taken by believers to mean that all of nature is derivative of god. The works of creation, being derivative, are usually deemed to be of lesser power and glory than their creator, in keeping with the important and widely diffused belief that a cause must always be of a higher potency than its effect.

Further, numbers of Christian commentators profess the belief that while the disobedience of Adam and Eve sullied the earth, the material world is nevertheless good and remains worthy of respect because god created it. In brief, what we call nature is viewed as the handiwork of god, not to be conflated with god. God stands apart from and transcends nature. As Werner Jaeger (1947:16–17) characterizes this Judeo-Christian point of view, the creation of the world "is a substantialization of an intellectual property or power of God the creator, who is stationed outside the world," and it contrasts with Greek ideas about gods who "are stationed inside the world … and are generated by the mighty power of Eros, who likewise belongs within the world as an all-engendering primitive force."

The Creator/Creature Classificatory Opposition

The salient conceptual opposition in Genesis and elsewhere in Hebrew scriptures (especially in Job) is between creatures and their radically transcendent creator, not between the natural and the supernatural. The Hebrew Bible supplies no distinct term that may be translated "supernatural" (Moshe Greenberg, personal communication). That, however, does not amount to sure evidence against the existence of a category of the supernatural inasmuch as covert categories or cryptotypes may sometimes be postulated in the absence of discrete labels. What is of greater moment here, however, is the actual classificatory structure expressed in the distinction between creator and creature and the uses made of that distinction.

The creator/creature distinction is all the more arresting when we contrast it to the natural/supernatural distinction popularly in use today. Many of our contemporaries assign god to the category "supernatural" along with angels (including fallen angels or demons), vampires, werewolves, witches, ghosts, spirits of the vasty deep, and much else.

Human beings and many other things, in contrast, are deemed "natural," not supernatural. Our contemporary popular classification, however, is not what is celebrated in Genesis 1. In that creation story, god stands alone. That is, god is the unique member of a distinct (if implicit) classificatory box, that of creator. In contrast, angels (good and bad), vampires, witches, ghosts, spirits of the vasty deep, their kindred and colleagues, as well as human beings, lions, tigers, bears, and all other created things mutually pertain to a different classificatory box, that of creatures. The classificatory conventions embedded in the biblical creation account, in short, differ from our contemporary, popular classificatory conventions.

The creator/creature distinction is not merely a classificatory artifact of a creation narrative. It is also a potent, generalized conceptual contrast, a crucial partitioning of presumed reality in the development of Jewish and Christian theologies. It had (and for some still has) applications. It was, for instance, invoked in the Arian controversy, a complex aggregate of evolving theological positions and arguments in fourth-century Christology.

Arius (c. 250–336 CE) maintained that Jesus Christ, although favored and elevated by god, was not really god—he did not, as it were, properly fit into the classificatory creator "box." Arius was quoted by his enemies as saying that "[t]here was a time when the Son was not," and that even if Christ be called god he "is not truly so, but by participation in grace he, as others, is god only in name" (Athanasius, *Orations against the Arians* 6 [PG 26:21–4]). The claim that Christ is a creature who, like other creatures, came into existence at some point in time, was rejected by the majority of churchmen who attended the Council of Nicaea in 325 CE. They adopted a statement affirming that Jesus Christ is "begotten, not made," that he is coeternal with the Heavenly Father, and that he is of the same substance as the Father, "true god from true god." In short, he is god and not a creature. And, in keeping with a strong and widely distributed determination to preserve monotheism while acknowledging the divinity of Jesus Christ, it was eventually accepted by many Christian theologians that Jesus Christ created the world, an understanding supported by the Doctrine of the Trinity.

Further developments in Christian theology relate in one way or another to the construction of the supernatural, and I sample several of them below.

Augustine of Hippo

Augustine of Hippo (354–430 CE), in *The City of God* (X, 12), holds that all creation—all nature—exists and perdures at god's pleasure. Indeed, all of nature represents god's abiding interest and continuing intervention in the world. Inasmuch as nature continues to exist at god's pleasure, and its existence manifests god's power, glory, and love, nature may be said to be miraculous, the product of an ongoing miracle.

Such a view would seem to rule out a sharply etched and stable natural/supernatural distinction. That is, by emphasizing nature as a continuing miracle, nature itself seems to approximate in some degree to what we moderns call "supernatural."

Theodore of Mopsuestia

Theodore of Mopsuestia (c. 350–428 CE) was a member of what some historians refer to as the Antioch School of Theology. Antioch (in present-day northern Syria) was a major Christian theological center in the fourth and fifth centuries of the Common Era. Theodore, one of that school's most illustrious members, is probably best remembered today for his arguments about what it means to say that Jesus Christ is both human and divine. His theological teachings on that topic relate to his ideas about human beings as a link between spiritual things and material things.

From at least the time of Aristotle (*The History of Animals* and other works), Euro-American intellectuals aspired to describe nature systematically. Many thought of it as a vast, inclusive hierarchy of different things, a hierarchy that metaphorically suggested a "Ladder of Nature" or a "Great Chain of Being" (Lovejoy 1936). Numbers of Stoic philosophers, for instance, so viewed it. Not surprisingly, many Christian intellectuals, in conceptualizing nature as a set of hierarchical arrangements, deemed those arrangements to be effects of divine causation. For that matter, ideas about divine causes and hierarchical natural effects were not only rife in the early centuries of the Common Era, but they persisted, and were variously modified and enhanced, in the Middle Ages, in the Renaissance, and well into modern times.

The Ladder of Nature consists of a number of conceptualized rungs or steps, those above being deemed superior in value as well as in position to those below. At the very bottom in some versions are rocks, stones, and dust, and at the very top is god. Each step incorporates important qualities of the step immediately below it while adding something considered to be superior. Thus, for instance, while rocks, stones, and dust have existence but no life, plants above them are credited with both existence and life.

Hierarchical rankings in value, moreover, are often attributed within classificatory rungs (except where the highest rung is occupied uniquely by god). Lions, for instance, are held to be superior to other wild animals, horses are judged superior to other domestic animals, and gold is thought to be superior to lead. In the Renaissance this logic is extended with various refinements to psychological and social distinctions, reason being valued over emotion, kings over nobles, nobles over peasants, and so forth.

With the development of modern science—particularly the biological sciences—the Great Chain of Being as an ordering construct lost much of its attraction among Euro-American intellectuals. Yet some of its features, and a vocabulary for discussing them, lingered on in the days of early modern science and later. Linnaeus's influential *Systema Naturae* (1737), for example, exhibits certain similarities to older classificatory hierarchies. And, by way of another example, Charles Lyell, the author of an influential pre-Darwinian scientific work (*Elements of Geology*, 1851), conceives of "missing links" in the geological record.

Theodore of Mopsuestia viewed nature—the totality of creation—as constituting a great chain of being threatened by its weakest link, sinful humanity. Like some Stoic philosophers and the Christian philosopher Nemesius of Emesa (1955), Theodore supposed that human beings are a vital connector in the universe, linking together its major parts. That is because, he believed, humans are the only creatures endowed by their creator with both spiritual and material qualities. They constitute links to the angels above them and to the beasts below them. The angels are pure spirit, pure intelligence. Animal nature, in contrast, has appetite but lacks soul and intelligence. Humans, who alone are both spiritual and material, bond together those major divisions of creation in accordance with the creator's great design. But their functional suitability for doing so is called into question by their sinful pride and disobedience.

In a worldview common among numbers of Christian intellectuals in the early fifth century, nature is neither dynamic (post-creation species do not emerge *de novo*) nor does it suffer the extinction of species. All forms are fixed until Judgment Day. But while there is ontological stability, functional stability is not thoroughgoing or absolute among creatures endowed with intelligence, especially as intelligence may be manifested in the exercise of free will. The exercise of free will, however, is freighted by the specifics of place in creation. Rebellious angels, for example, may detract from the serenity of creation, but, having been put in their place (so to speak), they are not in a position (literally or figuratively) to perturb further the divinely ordained order except by adding to the corruption of human beings. Corruptible and corrupted humankind, however, is another matter. In light of humanity's strategic position in the hierarchy of creation and its crucial bonding function, humans, having opted for sin, and being likely to continue opting for it, constitute a challenge to the divine design. Without reconciliation between god and humans, humankind casts a shadow on the integrity and continuation of god's creation. Such reconciliation, Theodore held, is affected by the redemptive mission of Jesus Christ.

We can interpret Theodore as further supposing that the redemptive mission of Christ renews and strengthens the bond between the spiritual and the material components of creation in two related ways.

First, as already pointed out, Theodore believed that Christ, by redeeming human beings from sin through his agony and death, effected a reconciliation between god and humans. Certain of the details bearing on Theodore's view of that reconciliation, however, are open to debate among contemporary historians. William C. Placher (1983:81) summarizes what is probably the most common interpretation of Theodore's position: that Jesus Christ was both fully human and fully divine, that he "saved humanity by uniting it with divinity," and that "only those parts of us which have been united with divinity in Christ will be saved." Frederick G. McLeod (2000), however, proffers a more complex and subtle interpretation of Theodore's position. McLeod attributes to Theodore an "unwavering conviction that God's transcendence can in no way be compromised," and he goes on to maintain that Theodore "does not see how the uncreated, infinite, and immutable Godhead can enter into a substantial union with a created, finite, and mutable human being in both this life and the next" (McLeod 2000:458). Although, according to McLeod, Theodore rejected the idea of a substantial union between god and human, he nevertheless supported the orthodox Christian view that Christ saves through his sacrifice of himself on the cross and his promise of life eternal, a promise vouchsafed by his resurrection. Furthermore, McLeod, like others, understands Theodore to hold that, in consequence of the redemption offered by Christ, saved humankind recapitulates its role as bond in god's creation.

Second, Christ himself serves both as universal bond and as the only true model of and for salvation in that he combines in one person (*prosōpon*) two natures (*phuseis*), the human and the divine. As Theodore puts it, god "renewed or rather, recapitulated in Christ" all the things of creation,

> those which are in heaven as well as those on earth, making, as it were, a certain vast renovation and reintegration, of every creature through him. For by making the body incorrupt and impassible by means of his resurrection and joining it again to the immortal soul ... he is seen to have restored the bond of friendship upon the entire creation.
>
> (quoted in McLeod 2000)

Two aspects of Theodore's position deserve further attention insofar as they may bear upon the development of the theological category of the supernatural. They are, respectively, Theodore's apparent "conviction that God's transcendence can in no way be compromised" and the limitation and consequential theological weakness of Theodore's position on Christ's two natures. McLeod is in all probability correct in maintaining that Theodore entertains a strong aversion to compromising the deity's transcendence.

But one can be ideologically opposed to compromise while inadvertently compromising. In deeming humankind a crucial bond in creation, Theodore attributes a cosmic significance—a cosmic importance—to our species. That importance would be conceptually enhanced were Christian intellectuals to adopt a further interpretive possibility: that humans are not simply an important bond in creation but a necessary one, conducing to the logical inference that their lapsed condition as sinners must be repaired lest creation somehow unravel. Theodore himself seems not to have gone that far, but the position that he espouses invites us to consider the possibility.

As I pointed out earlier in this chapter, many Euro-American theologians take theology to mean among other things the application of reason to lore about god or the gods, particularly with regard to the question of how divinity may impact our humanity. The interpretive possibility sketched above is a reasonable and relevant example of theologizing, and it certainly relates to what we know of Theodore's teachings. But it compromises god's transcendence. It does so by suggesting that a rational deity is logically obliged and motivated to do something to safeguard his creation. Indeed, merely by existing as a possible and plausible interpretive addendum to Theodore's theology it subverts the attribution to Theodore of an "unwavering conviction that God's transcendence can in no way be compromised." That sort of subversion, in my view, is inimical to the emergence and support of what became in medieval times the mainstream scholastic category of the supernatural, a theological category that asserts a transcendence of the natural order that is not subject to liens of any sort.

Theodore provides us with an example of how the rational implications of positive theological claims (kataphatic theology) may sometimes inadvertently compromise a theologian's theology. Theodore also provides us with an example of how theological positions may sometimes fail to win adherents because such positions are insufficiently bold (or, in the language of the cognitive science of religion, they are insufficiently counterintuitive).

Theodore of Mopsuestia is famous for his "two natures Christology." That is, Theodore maintained that Jesus Christ was both fully human and fully divine. As he put it, "[w]hen we try to distinguish the natures, we say that the person of the man is complete and that that of the Godhead is complete" (T-120, VIII-8). This doctrine went a long way toward resolving certain problems that concerned Christian theologians—but it didn't go far enough to resolve all of their concerns. In point of fact, the solution that Theodore worked out was "reasonable" in terms of the fundaments of two-valued, standard (Aristotelian) logic, but for many Christians it was theologically unsatisfying (especially among Theodore's most vociferous critics, certain theologians of the Alexandrian School).

Theodore, good logician that he was, held that each of Christ's natures had its own set of predicates. Thus when scriptures described Jesus as suffering and dying on the cross, the predicates in those descriptions were associated with his human nature (in keeping with the conviction that unchangeable deity does not suffer or die). And when scriptures described Jesus as raising Lazarus from the dead or performing other miracles, the relevant predicates related to his divine nature. This separation of predicates betokens standard logic.

Numbers of Christians, however, disliked and rejected Theodore's proffered solution. A principal reason had to do with their concerns about salvation. Inasmuch as they believed that their salvation depends on Christ's suffering and death, they further supposed that their salvation would be more secure if it were clearly warranted by the actual suffering and death of a god rather than that of a weak and malleable man.

Theodore's adherence to standard logic limited his theological options. An imaginative break with day-to-day logic might have been more successful. That proved to be the case in the developing theology of Cyril of Alexandria (c. 376–444 CE). Cyril was eventually canonized, and the Roman Catholic Church declared him to be one of its theological "Doctors," one of the great theologians in the history of Christendom. Theodore of Mopsuestia, in contrast, was proclaimed to be a heretic in an edict issued by the Emperor Justinian in 544, and in 553 the Fifth General Synod placed his person and his writings under anathema.

Starting his theological career with the opinion that Christ was one person and had one nature, Cyril eventually moved in the direction of claiming that Christ had two natures, the human and the divine. His final position, however, continued to suggest a certain caution or reticence in endorsing the claim of two natures. His caution may have been related in part to an awareness of the polysemy of the Greek term commonly used to speak about "nature." In Cyril's time *phúsis* variously meant nearly everything that exists (excepting god): divine creation; a collectivity of individuals of the same classificatory type (e.g., "human: nature"); an individual's state of being at birth, understood as a non-accidental set of developmental probabilities (in Latin *natura*, "nature," is related to *natus*, meaning "birth"); and a developed personal nature credited to a specific individual in distinguishing that individual from at least some other individuals of its type (e.g., "It is Tom's nature to do such and such"). The last listed meaning raised some problems for Cyril and for other Christian theologians when considered in tandem with the developing doctrine of the Trinity.

The doctrine of the Trinity in mainstream Christianity maintains that the godhead consists of three distinct persons who are mutually of one unique nature and who always act in perfect concert. That doctrine, however, does not stand alone. It is complemented by a mainstream doctrine respecting the Incarnation: that god so loved the world that the second person of the Trinity took on human flesh and dwelt among human beings. In debates about the details, however, Christian intellectuals sometimes recognized the need for creative theology lest the doctrine of the Incarnation, a doctrine that affirms the ontological and soteriological singularity of Jesus Christ, appears to transgress boundaries between the categories human and divine, boundaries that support the doctrine of the Trinity.

Most Trinitarian theologians by Cyril's time held that the second person of the Trinity, the son, was co-eternal with the heavenly father. Given the widespread Christian supposition that truly divine beings are not subject to change, the question arose as to whether or not god could really suffer and die on the cross—and if he could, how do we account for such a seeming departure from the nature of divine nature?

In what was perhaps a reaction to the recognition of multiple problematical possibilities, Cyril entered a claim that is in itself difficult to understand: that Christ "suffered impassibly"—that is, on first reading, that Christ suffered without suffering. What Cyril may have meant continues to be a topic for debate among theologians and historians. For example, a relatively recent interpretation that affirms Cyril's orthodoxy has been published by J. Warren Smith (2002). Smith begins in an interesting way. He begins not with the nature of divinity but with the nature of suffering. He suggests that Cyril supposed that while Christ as god did indeed suffer on the cross, he was not afflicted by the usual deleterious effects of suffering. In fine, according to Smith, Christ did not change in consequence of suffering (albeit he died, which I take to be a change). Smith, in any case, credits Cyril with believing what most other Christian theologians claim to believe: that Christ's suffering was not forced upon him by external forces to which he had to yield. His suffering, rather, was, voluntary (despite, or because of, an eleventh-hour prayer that he be spared the bitter cup of suffering and death).

The above discussion touches on some of the conceptual difficulties that Cyril encountered in his ongoing theological speculations about the nature of Christ. While he eventually came to accept the idea of two natures, the divine and the human, he remained reluctant to affirm their ontological separation sharply, preferring to write of "One nature united out of two." But if caution in his discursive accounts of the two natures may suggest a theological timidity or defensiveness, that was clearly not the case in his proffered resolution of the problem of how two natures in one person may relate functionally to one another. Cyril declared that the predicates associated with each nature also apply to the other. The technical Latin term for such an interchange of attributes is "*communicatio idiomatum*." Cyril's application of it served to assure many Christians who were concerned about their own salvation that not only did a man suffer and die on the cross, but so, too, did the Logos Incarnate. Cyril apparently held that this bold break with elemental (Aristotelian) logic was justified in the special case of Jesus Christ, the source of salvation. I deem it a brilliant example of how theology may sometimes be advanced by opting for the radically exceptional.

In resolving to his own satisfaction a major problem in Christology, Cyril also contributes to the emergence of the theological category of the supernatural. He declares that humans are elevated "above nature" or "beyond nature" (*hupèr phúsin*) through Christ (Kenny 1967:812). In Cyril's teachings, human beings who receive the salvation offered by Christ retain their created nature. Cyril does not maintain that humans enter into a substantial union with god. Like other supporters of Athanasian theology, he holds that the Father, Son, and Holy Spirit share the same uniquely divine substance. Humans, Cyril opines, do not come to share that substance. But humans can enter into a fellowship with the godhead that is conceptually and experientially similar to, but not the same thing as, the union of love that the Father, Son, and Spirit share. Modeled on the reciprocal love of the three divine persons, humans become adoptive children of god by participating in god's grace.

Cyril's teachings include a remarkably simple-seeming supernaturalist vocabulary—principally the expression *hupèr phúsin*—for talking about the soteriological process and its culmination. Once we begin to unpack the idea of elevation "above/beyond nature," however, we see that the verbal expression that encapsulates it is open to interpretation and can convey quite a lot.

In the orthodox Christian theology that Cyril (among others) was instrumental in establishing, salvation is claimed not only to correct the lapsed condition of sinners, but in other respects to effect a transformation in the creature. Christian theologians, however, differ on the particulars. Virtually all agree that salvation conduces to life eternal, a triumph over death, "the last enemy." And many also opine that the transformative process that elevates humans above nature secures the "divinization" of humans and the seeing of god. This, as scholastic theologians describe it later, is the *ens supernaturalis*, the supernatural end, the supernatural fulfillment, of human life. But here as elsewhere there is a notable elasticity in speculating about the details.

Divinization: The Supernatural End

In developing his theology of grace, Cyril built upon some of the ideas that other Church Fathers proffered. Cyril, moreover, was somewhat more conservative in use of language than some of his predecessors. Thus, for instance, Irenaeus of Lyon (*c.* 130–200 CE) declared that the Word of God, "through his transcendent love, became what we are, that he might bring us to be even what he is himself" (*Against Heresies*, Book 5, Preface).

Clement of Alexandria (*c.* 150–215 CE) wrote that "[t]he Word of God became man so that you may learn from him how man may become God" (*Exhortation to the Heathen*, chapter 1). And Athanasius of Alexandria (*c.* 296–373 CE), probably the most influential Christian theologian of his time, is on record as saying that the Son "was made man so that we might be made God" (*On the Incarnation* 54:3), although in his *Discourse against the Arians* 3.10, he remarks that "to become as the Father is impossible for us creatures, who have been brought to be out of nothing."

"Divinization" is a complex topic, but an important one for our understanding of the development of the theological category of the supernatural. First of all, as the quotations furnished above indicate, there is a measure of ambiguity in what early Christian theologians say about it. Some talk about humans becoming god whereas others write about humans becoming god-like. Not only that, but an individual's actual statements may vary somewhat over time, as in the above-cited case of Athanasius. And then, of course, there is the problem of fathoming what it may mean to say that a human becomes god or god-like.

Some Christians seem to interpret statements about becoming god as entailing little or no theological difference with statements about becoming god-like. Others, however, perceive significant differences, differences that entail problems—such as, for instance, the problem of whether or not an ontological transformation in the human, a transformation in substance or "nature," is imputed in statements about "man becoming god." Augustine of Hippo pointed to a further complexity when, in a sermon (*Sermo 13 de Tempore*: PL39, 1097–8), he preached, "My brethren, what miracles! What prodigies! The laws of nature are changed in the case of man"—as, indeed, they would be were humans truly to escape death. Further, there are subtle but real problems in translating religious beliefs and theological doctrines about divinization from one language to another—how, for instance, should we translate into English Thomas Aquinas's assertion in Latin, *Solus deus deificet*? "god alone makes god-like?" Or "god alone deifies" (that is, "god alone makes one into god")?

Early Christian assertions that a human person may become god or god-like usually relate to three predicates widely accepted by Christian theologians in describing god: that god is deathless, that god is impassible (not subject to suffering or change), and that god is incorruptible (not subject to decay or loss of vigor). These three predicates also apply to humans who are said to be divinized. For early Christian theologians, indeed, the three predicates, when applied to human beings, are basic statements about the end product of the salvific process. (Later theologians, such as Thomas Aquinas, add to the complexity of that process by introducing additional considerations.)

Now, deathlessness, impassibility, and incorruptibility were also cited indications of divinity among the classical Greeks. In Greek literature, moreover, those qualities were sometimes extended by the gods (or by Zeus in particular) to favored human beings. Yet while both pagan Greek religion and early Christian theology incorporated ideas about immortality, impassibility, and incorruption and their extension to human beings, they differed in the respective conceptual contexts and emotional tones associated with those indications of divinity.

Among the Greeks, positive cathexis was strongest and most evident in the hero cults and in the later mystery religions; strong emotional investment appeared to be less striking in other components of Greek thought, which was often more worldly than other-worldly. For many Christians in the early centuries, however, soteriology was of absorbing and fervent interest. While both the pagan Greeks and the early Christians affirmed beliefs of the sort that modern students of religion call "supernatural beliefs," enthusiasm for divinization and other aspects of salvation was more salient among Christians than among pagan Greeks. And Christian enthusiasm fueled the emergence of a distinctly Christian theological category of the supernatural.

Everything was in place: a creator outside of and superior to nature; a savior who is both fully human and fully divine and who suffered and died to effect the reconciliation of creature and creator; and the divinization, the supernaturalizing, not merely of small numbers of heroes but of all those who believe in the salvation offered by Christ. What was missing was an established vocabulary that would solidify and expand on the classificatory structure that was already in place: the biblically rooted distinction between creator and creature; the ancillary classificatory contrast between nature as creation and that which surpasses it; and the triumph of rising above the course of nature by transcending death, suffering, and corruption. We find, moreover, a nascent vocabulary and way of speaking among early Christians. I supply some examples in the preceding pages, with special attention to Cyril of Alexandria's use of the Greek expression *hupèr phúsin*, a verbal formulation that signals the emergence of a theology of the supernatural. In its subsequent development, moreover, that theology eventually acquired greater conceptual and terminological sophistication. Curiously enough, one source of sophistication proved to be a pagan philosophical tradition—the Neoplatonism of Late Antiquity—that expressed misgivings about the clarity and other powers of natural language predicates for describing divine reality.

The Neoplatonism of Late Antiquity

"Neoplatonism" is a term that modern Western scholarship assigns to philosophies that it deems extensions of Plato's philosophy. While sometimes using Platonic texts for lengthy exegeses (typically offered as commentaries on discrete works), the different Neoplatonisms are individuated in part by departing from Plato in their own ways (as, for instance, in the case of some late Neoplatonisms appropriately and generically labeled "Christian Neoplatonism"). My concern here is with the Neoplatonisms of Late Antiquity: philosophies expounded in Greek by authors who lived in the third through sixth centuries of the Common Era. Modern scholars generally agree that major figures in that tradition include Plotinus (*c.* 205–270 CE), Porphyry (*c.* 233–303 CE), Iamblichus (*c.* 245–325 CE), and Proclus (410–485 CE), all of whom were pagans.

The Neoplatonisms of Late Antiquity are strongly marked examples of a predilection encountered in ancient (Archaic and Classical) Greek philosophy. That is, a focus on ontology.

My judgment in that regard is relative to what I take to be a modernist and contrasting predilection, a preference for epistemology. In modern times, indeed, some intellectuals express strong disdain for ontology in that, in their opinions, it fails to contribute reliably to modernist efforts to understand ourselves in coming to understand other people and the world. Thus, for instance, the biologist Steve Jones (1997:1314) identifies "philosophy" with what he calls the interpretation of nature "in metaphysical terms," and he opines that for most scientists "philosophy is to science as pornography is to sex: it is cheaper, easier, and some people seem, bafflingly, to prefer it." Yet a modernist preference to deconstruct what some take to be ontological terms (e.g., "religion")—or to do away with them entirely—may well encourage us to convert all-too-simplistically ontological issues into epistemological ones, and by so doing to narrow our understandings.

On the other extreme, the strong preference of the Neoplatonisms of Late Antiquity for ontology accounts in part for the difficulties some of us moderns experience in reading their texts. We are not on their wavelength, and the neophyte may well exclaim, "What in the world is Plotinus (or Iamblichus, or so-and-so) talking about?" Interestingly enough, Plotinus and his metaphysical kin are talking about what the Milesian philosophers in Chapter 2 are usually said to be talking about: how the many different things of our universe ultimately derive from one primal reality, the one becoming many. While, however, we have very little to go on as to what else the Milesians may have claimed, we have quite a lot to read (and digest) in the case of the Neoplatonists of Late Antiquty. For the contemporary proponent of the cognitive science of religion, the most attention-getting aspects of those Neo-Platonic writings include their cosmogenic, cosmological, and theological claims on the one hand and the posited intuitive faculties of our "souls" for grasping ontologies on the other hand. An entry into some of what they claim is afforded by a consideration of "emanationism."

Emanationism

The English word "emanate" comes from the Latin *emanare*, to flow from, to flow out of. Emanationist cosmogonies and cosmologies typically posit a transcendent Absolute or "First Principle" from which all else flows (emanates), including what we call the natural world as identified by its processes. The philosophical doctrine undergirding emanationism is usually "immanent causation," the idea that effects are contained or implicit within their causes.

For Plotinus and numbers of other emanationists, sensibles exist within intelligibles, and intelligibles are their causes (for a basic distinction between sensibles and intelligibles, see the discussion of Plato in Chapter 2). As Wallis (1972:102) puts it with respect to the Neoplatonic cosmogonies of Late

Antiquity, the universe is conceptualized as "a spontaneous production of the Intelligible order, with no question of an anthropomorphic creator of all." From Plotinus's point of view, an understanding of nature is best achieved through the exercise of what Sara Rappe (2000:xiv) calls "the faculty of intellectual intuition." She goes on to say (2000:44) that "Plotinus suggests that the world can be seen as from within the mind." Or, as John Herman Randall, Jr., puts it,

> Plotinos takes "Thought" as the primary fact of experience, "Thought" as a noun, as a finished logical system. He interprets existence in terms of such Thought and its structure. Our own scientific procedures and values make us prefer to take existence as primary, and to interpret thought in terms of existence. That is, Plotinos is making a logical analysis of the logical structure and conditions of existence; he is obviously not a natural scientist analyzing physical causes and consequences.
>
> (Randall, Jr. 1970:122)

This overall philosophical perspective fails to offer the promise of what we normally understand by the terms "social relationship" or "personal relationship" as imagined between ourselves (our souls, according to Plotinus) and the source of all being. Social or personal "relationships," that is, are distinct from, say, the impersonal implications that our scientists postulate between attractors and what they attract.

For Plotinus, the source of all being, the One (*to hen*), is beyond being and beyond the other predicates of natural languages (see the discussion of "negative theology" that follows this section). The One both emanates and attracts. Thus the human soul or *psúchē*, which emanates from the World Soul, which emanates from Intellect (*nous*), which emanates from the One, is also drawn toward union with the One. Plotinus imagines that humans are innately disposed to enjoy union with god (*Enneads* V.1.11.14; Rappe 2000:3, n.3). The experience of union through contemplation, indeed, is signaled by an ecstasy said to be impossible to describe (Porphyry, *Life of Plotinus*, tells us that Plotinus probably achieved union four times during the six years that Porphyry was with him).

Contemplative union, although likely to be especially appealing to intellectuals, is not the same thing as a sustainable and sustained social relationship initially understood in terms of human models. Nor does it point to anything in the way of a personal nature or personal attributes that can be credited to the One. Contemplative union differs in those respects from what some Christian theologians claim to be the fulfillment of a natural human longing for the supernatural as signaled by desire for the Beatific Vision and participation in the divine nature. Although the Beatific Vision and Mystical Union are also likely to be particularly attractive to intellectuals, their attainment, according to some theologians, is said to raise the human mind to new understandings, thus perhaps reducing intellectual disparities by elevating all saved human minds. In any case, numbers of Christian theologians affirm that realization of the Beatific Vision and Mystical Union are made possible by the supernatural gift of wholly gratuitous grace, an unmerited gift conferred by a loving god on his human creatures. The supernatural gift of grace, they claim, makes possible a relationship of love between creature and creator that is modeled on the loving relationship among the three divine persons of the Trinity. There is really nothing comparable in the teachings of Plotinus.

The absence in Plotinus's schema of what we ordinarily conceive of as a social relationship may be of special interest to contemporary social scientists, and particularly those who endorse the anthropologist Robin Horton's characterization of religion. "Religion," Horton writes, "can be looked upon as an extension of the field of people's social relationships beyond the confines of purely human society" (1960:211). In comparing the historical trajectories of Neoplatonism and Christianity and the roads that led to and from the theological category of the supernatural, the presence or absence of an emphasis on social relationships (as distinguished from an emphasis on attractors and what they attract) may well eclipse in consequences other engineering aspects of world-making.

Let us compare, for instance, the Christian theologian Theodore of Mopsuestia to Plotinus in the matter of a social relationship between god and human. Theodore, it may be recalled, deems his god to so transcend humanity that, according to McLeod (2000:458), a substantial union between god and humans is "impossible." (Impossible, it seems, in Durkheim's sense.) Yet Theodore, as is the case for numbers of other Christian theologians, supposes that "all things are possible to god" (thus suggesting a need for paradox-aversive explications of logical considerations in discussing divinity). In any case, while Theodore holds that god definitively transcends all creation, he also holds that personal relationships between god and humans are both possible and desirable. In his case, the allowance for personalism is modeled in part on Theodore's theological claims about the union of divine nature and human nature in the person of Jesus Christ.

The emphasis on a social relationship between god and human in Christian creedal, theological, and ritual engagements is of considerable historical significance. Along with a large number of other things (such as social welfare networks, ecclesiastical structures modeled on serviceable Roman political institutions, the promise of life eternal, etc.), an emphasis on social relationships helps account for the appeal and spread of Christianity. In contrast, and even though Plotinus's brand of Neoplatonism displays some religion-like aspects and elements, its highly cerebral complexity and coolness and its fundamental impersonality render it a philosophy of more limited attraction. Subsequent forms of Neoplatonism in late antiquity enlarged the field of attractors, in part by incorporating theurgic elements, magical claims, and practices that were probably valued by some for their mystery as well as for their promise. But theurgic attractors, in my opinion, did not equal the widespread appeals of Christian communion, of fellowship claimed to be between god and human and that served as an idealized model for a human moral community, a human moral community that Durkheim called a "church." If anything, the limited social attractions and impress of theurgy in the Neoplatonism of late antiquity could be interpreted as validating one of Durkheim's most famous general claims: "There is no Church of Magic!" The differential attractions of Neoplatonism and Christianity notwithstanding, Neoplatonism did make some contributions to the advancement of a theological category of the supernatural.

Negative Theology

Negative theology of one sort or another is advocated in some non-Western cultural traditions as well as in the West, probably most famously in what we call Hinduism (Coward 1992; Koller 1982:102–3). And the *via negativa* or "negative way" has been brilliantly (and controversially) addressed in our time by the French philosopher and deconstructionist Jacques Derrida (see, for example, a collection of essays—some by Derrida, others about him—edited by Harold Coward and Toby Foshay 1992). I limit discussion of negative theology in this work, however, to a small number of Euro-American cases that bear on the emergence and development of the theological category of the supernatural.

The term "negative theology" is often described in Euro-American dictionaries and other sources as if it were fully synonymous with the expression "apophatic theology" (from the Greek *apophēmi*, to deny).

Apophatic theology pivots on an axiomatic claim: that all of the predicate terms of natural languages are inadequate and potentially misleading when used to describe divine reality. Proponents are likely to maintain, for instance, that the statement "god is wise" cannot be properly understood in the same way as the statement "Socrates is wise." Indeed, "god is wise" is not really to be understood at all except, perhaps, as a crude and misleading analogy, for god is wise in a way appropriate only to god. Since god transcends everything, numbers of theologians, say, our finite human minds, cannot truly fathom his nature and attributes. We are better off, some suggest, to limit ourselves to stating what god is not, to denying that he is such and such (apophatic theology), rather than attempting to state what he is (kataphatic theology).

We might call this point of view "negative theology lite." What I call "negative theology heavy" is a logical position that rejects apophatic theology as well as kataphatic theology. Rejection of both, if actually recommended, is likely to be called for by those who maintain that god encompasses all possibilities, including opposites. Those who might hold that opinion, moreover, would tend to suppose that any contrary opinion, if true, would diminish god. That is, to posit a god that does not encompass all possibilities is to posit a god of lesser ontological completeness than one who does.

Now, if god (for the sake of argument) were indeed to encompass all possibilities including opposites, both apophatic and kataphatic theology would prove unsatisfactory. They would be unsatisfactory because, at their very best, they respectively affirm only half-truths. The transcendent truth, according to this point of view, is that god is both what he is and what he is not. When we combine that "truth" with a sense of ourselves as cognitively limited, we may well conclude that we cannot truly understand god through the collaboration of our intellects with the resources provided by our languages. We might therefore try, some propose, to understand the divine by direct experience of it—that is, as I pointed out elsewhere, through mystical engagements. Both light and heavy negative theology have historically supported mystical aspirations and advocacies and, at the very least, de facto supernaturalism.

4

Something Nice about Vampires

What is nice about vampires?

Some vampires appear to be as nasty and as diabolical as Van Helsing maintains. But virtually all vampires, good and evil, are rule-governed, and that renders them "nice"—which is to say, predictable, to some degree.

Vampires may or may not be obliged to spend the daylight hours in their coffins. Or, like Le Fanus's *Carmilla*, they may or may not sleep on a bed of blood. Or they may or may not fear contact with running water.

Or they may recoil from certain religious icons. And so on. Vampiric niceties may take different shapes and favor different behaviors. But, for the most part, and speaking generally, there are vampiric behaviors and the ontologies that distinguish them from virtually all else, if only to some extent.

Not only do some anthropologists and other students of religion continue to disagree among themselves about the definitions of key terms, but they argue about whether or not we should abandon efforts to define "religion" as an analytical term. Some scholars explicitly dismiss "religion" and/or "supernatural" as justifiable categories, or they otherwise claim not to need them (e.g., Timothy Fitzgerald 2000).

Now, while the term "supernatural" often relates to the term "religion" in Euro-American discourses, we cannot legitimately claim that all objects or events dubbed "supernatural" are "religious." As noted earlier, some living things are diverting or entertaining or they answer to still other needs, and they are popularly accepted as such (e.g., Bram Stoker's "Dracula").

Present-day cognitive and evolutionary scientists generally hold that the supernatural often rests on beliefs about the reality, functions, and variable imaginings of counterintuitive (or minimally counterintuitive) ontologies. They usually maintain, moreover, that those beliefs and the mental machineries that process them are broadly similar to those encountered in ordinary or "natural" life.

Nevertheless, in a stripped-down characterization of some of what is involved, various contemporary students of religion suppose that supernatural agents are often hallmarks of religion. Indeed, they maintain that religious belief is typically belief in the existence and activities of counterintuitive agents. The voteries of such agents, that is, are typically credited with understandings of, or beliefs in, counterintuitive properties such as invisibility, superhuman strength, immortality, and so forth.

While my general claims about counterintuitivity are inherited, so to speak, from Pascal Boyer, it should be noted that there is also something of a scholarly debate in process regarding the matter of minimalism as well. Some scholars deem it important to claim that successful religious beliefs—beliefs, that is, that are passed on from one generation to the next—are often beliefs that are minimally counterintuitive.

In any case, the term "intuitive" generally means to suppose or to understand something in the absence of discrete ratiocinations, distinct data, and/or explicit instructions. The counterintuitive, broadly put, is contrary to what we intuitively expect.

While the counterintuitive is associated with many ideas, including some generated by modern science and its subversions of naive realism, it is especially noteworthy in religion and the supernatural.

Religious representations and the supernatural often violate people's ideas of what commonly takes place in their environments (Boyer 1994:48). Not only do religious representations often violate many intuitive expectations, but, as Boyer (1994) argues, religious notions would probably not be as interesting or as attention demanding as they are if they complied with intuitions about ordinary events and states.

Boyer (1994:48) supposes that the sorts of religious ideas that are most likely to be transmitted from generation to generation, that are most likely to prove successful in ideational competitions, are those that strike "an optimal cognitive balance" between the intuitive and the counterintuitive. Their intuitiveness, their harmony with expectations supported by ordinary ontological commitments, renders them feasible and learnable. But their violations of such expectations, their seeming "ontological unnaturalness," as Boyer puts it, renders them "attention demanding."

Now, in addition to their efforts to account for transmissions of religious ideas, cognitive scientists of religion and the supernatural are concerned with finding and explaining recurrent features in the representations and meta-representations of different cultures.

Contemporary scholars recognize that there are similarities between religious ideas in many human populations, and such similarities are often a matter of family resemblances (Boyer 1994:5). Explaining recurrences in religious ideas and behaviors among the world's population, however, sometimes involve us in subtleties that go beyond the recognition and coding of resemblances.

An example of what I have in mind can be drawn from my fieldwork and that of others among the Wayuu, an Amerindian population of northern Colombia and Venezuela. A term utilized in the local language is "*pülasü.*" *Pülasü* is sometimes used to mean "mysterious," as in the sentence "I dreamed last night of mysterious (or unknown) persons." Sometimes, however, *pülasü* can be said to mean "mysteriously harmful," as if mysterious things are usually or potentially harmful. Wayuu who receive such messages (often in dreams) come close to what Euro-Americans mean by supernatural. But there are interpretive grades. Not every use of *pülasü* signals harm, but many do.

In any case, increasing our understandings of religion and the supernatural is likely to improve our sensitivities at various levels. In yesteryear anthropologists tended to emphasize the distinctiveness of the peoples they studied and the powers of culture in, as Ruth Benedict put it, the "molding" of human behavior. Anthropological scholars of earlier times were given, that is, to emphasizing culture as that which molds behavior. That was (and to some extent still is) a popular bias, compatible with the somewhat dubious claim that anthropology is "The Study of Culture," or "The Science of Culture," or something of the sort rather than the more inclusive "Study of Human Beings."

Today's scholars, or at least those who champion the cognitive science of religion and its many expressions in supernatural worlds, appear to be bolder both in hypothesizing about the world and testing internal structures than were the scholars of old. While anthropologists today continue to be aware of cultural differences and distinctions, those who operate under the banners of the cognitive and evolutionary sciences of religion and their associated investments in the supernatural strike me as being generally more intrigued by the explanatory possibilities of innateness than were their predecessors and some of their present-day successors.

And that, I suppose, is often to the good!

5

Dracula and Carmilla: Monsters and the Mind

Introduction

Following the publication of Bram Stoker's *Dracula* in 1897, vampire narratives proliferated in Britain and the United States. While many twentieth-century short stories, novels, plays, and films in both countries depart from *Dracula* in various ways, it is our impression that *Dracula* and its close derivatives retain pride of place in the popular imagination. Yet *Dracula* was but one of several well-known vampire stories published in English during the nineteenth century, and scholars deem certain of the other tales to be of literary merit.

In noting that, we raise this question: What is it about the plot and the characterization of vampires in *Dracula* that make it the most famous example of vampires in English fiction? Why, in particular, has it been more influential than Le Fanu's *Carmilla* (1872), which preceded it in time and is of equal or perhaps greater literary distinction? We address that question, and by doing so we hope to gain some insight into the attraction and persistence of vampire tales across time and cultures.

"Prototype"

We begin by sketching our approach to conceptualizing the category "vampire." Nina Auerbach, Professor of English at the University of Pennsylvania, writes that "[t]here is no such creature as 'The Vampire'; there are only vampires" (1995:5). That declaration is in keeping with her demonstration that in nineteenth- and twentieth-century British and American vampire novels, short stories, plays, and films, vampires vary greatly in behavior, in apparent motivation, and in cultural significance. Different social orders and different culturally supported sensibilities and sensitivities, she persuasively argues, find expression in different sorts of vampires.

We deem Auerbach's literary nominalism preferable to an essentialism that would govern vampiric class inclusion by insisting on some conjunction of necessary features or conditions. At the same time, however, we think that there is a better way of allowing for differences in conceptualizing vampires and in understanding their multifaceted significance in British and American imaginings of the last two centuries. That way combines the recognition of family resemblances with insights derived from prototype theory in the cognitive sciences.

A family resemblance approach can be quite liberal in what it includes as instantiations of the category "vampire." It can encompass not only such familiar (albeit different) figures as Ruthven, Varney, Carmilla, Dracula, and Lestat, but also others, including so-called psychic vampires, who flourish by draining vitality, will, and even experience from their victims. But, it may be asked, does this not create a category that is so promiscuous in what it includes as to render the category analytically useless? No, we reply, once you couple family resemblance with insights from prototype theory.

Prototype theory, narrowly described, attempts to account for "prototype effects." Prototype effects are differences in the judgments that people render about how well different instances of a category exemplify the category. Thus, for instance, many people judge apples and oranges to be clearer or better exemplars of the category "fruit" than olives, and robins and sparrows to be clearer or better exemplars of the category "bird" than penguins. Judgments can be explicitly given, or they can be inferred from the order of examples that people give or from their responses to lists of examples furnished by others. Prototype theorists call the adjudged clearest or "best" examples of categories "prototypes" or "the most prototypical exemplars" (Lakoff 1987; Rosch 1978:36). This approach celebrates centrality and periphery rather than essence and boundary in conceptualizing categories (Saler 2000). It allows that some instantiations of a category may be deemed more central to the category than others. Thus in the case of vampires, Dracula is more central to the category than, say, the shape-shifting space alien who extracts salt from victims in an episode of *Star Trek, First Generation*. That centrality is recognized by Auerbach (1995:111) when she refers to "Dracula's dominance in our century." We contend, moreover, that while Sheridan Le Fanu's vampire Carmilla is more prototypical—that is, an adjudged better exemplar of the category— than vampiric space aliens and legions of psychic vampires, she is less prototypical than Bram Stoker's Count Dracula.

Our Argument

We attempt to support and extend the above contention by means of a two-stage argument. First, we maintain that Stoker's novel *Dracula* is more prototypical than *Carmilla* because its narrative features conform fully to the general structure of widely encountered monster-slaying stories whereas that is not the case for *Carmilla*. Second, we suggest that the monster-slaying narrative structure of which the novel *Dracula* is an example is itself both warranted by, and an expression of, the evolved architecture of the human mind. We take each in turn.

Monster-Slaying Stories

In contemporary English the word "monster" is used in a variety of ways. In applying it to folk narratives, however, we can productively limit its range. We commonly use it to refer to legendary or mythical beings in narratives that display, to greater or lesser extents, certain family resemblances. The anthropologist David Gilmore has sampled monsters described in the folk narratives of diverse cultures and represented in paintings and sculpture from the Upper Paleolithic to the present. He finds that monsters typically exhibit a constellation of features: great size and/or remarkable strength; a prominent mouth with fangs or some other means of facilitating predation on humans; a cannibalistic urge to consume human flesh and/or blood; and hybridism, for they often combine human and animal features, or mix living and dead tissue, or manifest amalgams of discordant parts of various organisms (Gilmore 2003:174–89).

Elaborations on, and discriminations among, monster traits can be found in folklorist Stith Thompson's 1964 tale-type index as well as in his 1955 catalog of motifs encountered in thousands of folk narratives from around the world. Both list monster elements that remind us of Dracula and other highly prototypical vampires. For example: monster drinks blood of human prey; person transformed into monster; monster cannot endure daylight; monster is powerless after cockcrow; and monster is unable to cross a stream.

More broadly with respect to narrative organization, Gilmore maintains that monster tales exhibit "a recurring structure no matter what the culture or setting" (2003:13). That is, we find in monster tales a characteristic three-stage, repetitive cycle.

First, the monster emerges from mysterious nether regions, much to the surprise and consternation of some human community. Second, the monster attacks and kills humans, and early attempts of the victims to defend themselves fail. Third, the community is saved by a culture hero who, by his strength and wit, contrives to defeat the monster. This cycle is likely to repeat itself for, if the monster is driven away, it returns, and, if it is slain, its kin may later appear.

We supplement Gilmore's analysis by noting that the monster-slaying hero is often cognitively advantaged over those whom he saves. He assumes that the monster's behavior is rule-governed, and he knows or infers the rules and uses his grasp of them to advantage. He thus exhibits admirable meta-representational skills, for by forming predictive representations of the monster's representations, he is better able to dispatch it. We claim that in Stoker's novel *Dracula* the characterization of vampires strongly resembles that of typical folkloric monsters. We maintain, moreover, that the plot of Stoker's novel replicates the three-stage structure of typical folkloric monster-slaying tales. The English vampire stories that preceded it in the nineteenth century either fail to create vampires that are folkloric monsters, or they fail to include most of the plot elements found in the structure of typical monster tales or both. While Le Fanu's tale *Carmilla* comes close in certain ways to emulating folkloric characterization and plot, it must nevertheless be accounted a failure in that regard for the following three reasons.

First, as Auerbach (1995) plausibly argues, the vampire Carmilla and her best-known predecessors are primarily motivated by a desire for intimacy with a human, and the need to feed on blood is secondary. This, however, is not the case for Count Dracula (Auerbach 1995:64) or for the typical monster of folklore as characterized by Gilmore (2003). In motivation and the likely multivalent responses to that motivation on the part of readers, the vampire Carmilla can be accounted less "monstrous" than Stoker's unambiguously evil Count. While readers may pity and perhaps even feel some liking or sympathy for Carmilla, as well as a physical attraction to her, they are less likely to do so in the case of Stoker's creation.

Second, there is Dracula's animality, a feature that reminds us of the hybrid monsters of folklore. Not only does he have hair on his palms, but he transforms into a canine, a bat, and even fog and mist (Auerbach 1995:86).

While Le Fanu hints at the possibility that Carmilla may take cat form, he characteristically blurs that possibility, in keeping with the ambiguity that pervades his narrative. In other respects, however, Carmilla is too beautiful by human standards, too romantically ethereal, and too appealingly erotic to suggest discordant or repulsive shape-shifting or other physically distasteful folkloric markers of the unambiguously monstrous, at least when compared to the hairy, foul-smelling, and in other respects physically unpleasant Count.

Third, Stoker's novel *Dracula* is a self-contained monster-slaying story that provides closure and catharsis. The intrusion of the supernatural into the natural is successfully resisted, in large measure in consequence of Van Helsing's revelation that the supernatural is rule-governed (albeit by special rules) and that a knowledge of the rules appropriate to vampires gives us power over them. Indeed, by the end of Stoker's novel loose ends are tied and boundaries are restored. But this is not the case for Le Fanu's novelette *Carmilla*. As Jack Sullivan (1978:60) points out, *Carmilla* "does not have a neat resolution in which evil is banished." It is a tale distinguished by its "openendedness and irresolution." Some characters—the woman who claims to be Carmilla's mother, her coachmen, and the mysterious black woman—appear and then are heard of no more. Carmilla's fate, once she is dispatched as a vampire, is unclear, and we are left with the unresolved possibility that Laura may not be free of vampirism. In *Carmilla*, Sullivan (1978:64) writes, "Ambivalence is the controlling principle throughout the story." But that is not true of typical monster-slaying narratives.

Monsters and the Mind

Now, if you accept our claim that *Dracula* is the most prototypical of English vampire tales because it was the first among its nineteenth-century companions to conform fully to the typical characterization and plot of monster-slaying narratives, then we are obliged to account in some way for the power of such narratives in human imaginings. Gilmore (2003:135) affirms that "a deep and abiding fascination with monsters is pancultural." Why should that be? David Quammen, the author of a recent book on predators, suggests that we look to our evolutionary past for an answer:

> Great and terrible flesh-eating beasts have always shared landscape with humans. They were part of the ecological matrix within which *Homo sapiens* evolved. The big teeth of predators, their ferocity, and their hunger, were grim realities that could be eluded but not forgotten. Every once in a while, a monstrous carnivore would emerge from forest or river to kill someone and feed on the body. And it conveyed a certain message. Among the earliest forms of human self-awareness was the awareness of being meat.
> (Quammen 2003:1)

Recent work by certain anthropologists on ideation allows us to explore further the suggestion that the answer lies in our evolutionary past. The anthropologists to whom we refer draw not only on the ethnographic and ethnological findings of their own discipline but also on the cognitive and neural sciences, evolutionary biology, and developmental and evolutionary psychology.

One such anthropologist, Pascal Boyer (2001:216), points to the fact that "[h]umans and their hominid ancestors have been both predators and prey for a very long time" (see also Bloch 1992). Given, indeed, our long history as prey, it is reasonable to suppose that among our ancestors, as in the case of various other animals that were also threatened with becoming "meat," selection occurred for neurologically grounded dispositions to apperceive, and to respond to, predatory threats. Frequently encountered responses among prey species include flight, fight, or playing-dead.

On the human level, as many of the anthropologists to whom we refer suppose, apperception of predatory threats relates to a hypothesized mental "module" or set of modules. In the current modular theory of mind (see, e.g.,

Hirschfeld and Gelman 1994), such modules, viewed dynamically, can be broadly characterized as involving two sorts of functions: first, sensitivities to informational inputs that vary from module to module (inputs can stem from perceptual apparatuses, from the outputs of other modules, or from both); second, dispositions to operate on inputs in determinate ways. Thus, by way of a hypothesized and somewhat simplified example, a predator-sensitivity module would register or process cues about the presence of predators and trigger appropriate behavior and certain emotional responses associated with such behavior.

Sometimes false positives occur, as when, for example, a rock formation is mistaken for a large carnivore. But even more interesting with respect to contemporary human populations, vicarious positives may occur. That is, we can vicariously and empathetically experience the sense of danger and other emotions triggered as part of predation avoidance or confrontation while overriding impulses to engage in actual fight, flight, or playing-dead behaviors. Many of the readers of these lines have done so in the relative safety of motion-picture theaters.

The modular theory of mind envisions a large number of possible modules for different domains of human experience. While predation-sensitivity would appear to be comparatively direct and seemingly "automatic" (except when overridden in whole or in part), some other hypothesized modules implicate comparatively complex and subtle inference systems, inference systems that can sometimes be rendered even more complex and subtle from established personal and cultural archives of ontological understandings and expectations. Indeed, as Boyer (2001:226) suggests, "Once a particular object or theme triggers rich inferences in a variety of mental systems, it is more likely to be the object of great cultural attention and elaboration."

Now, since monsters, in one form or another, were an omnipresent feature of our evolutionary past, tales about *slaying* monsters, which trigger inferences associated with predation and "fight" rather than "flight" or "playing-dead," have a salience and relevance for us that represent a heritage from our Paleolithic ancestors. That salience and relevance, we contend, accounts for the continued invention and re-invention of such tales in the plenitude of cultures known to us from the Paleolithic to the present. We fear monsters—vicarious fear is still fear—and we derive pleasure—vicarious pleasure is still pleasure—from killing them. The psychological stress occasioned by our fear is relieved by the slaying, and the reductive process is experienced as pleasurable.

Feelings of pleasure derived from monster-slaying tales, moreover, may be associated with the phenomenon of "play." Play is defined here as autogenous behavior observed in the juveniles of many animal species, including the human. While such play may seem to be frivolous in the sense of not being directly connected to survival needs, numbers of theorists argue that it indirectly enhances survival prospects. It does so by rehearsing (and thus training for) important future roles (as, for example, in the stalking behavior of kittens). Humans are given to greater varieties and complexities of play than other animals. In addition, and in greater degree than what is found among other animals, human play occurs, and is sometimes rather intense, in maturity. Humans, moreover, differ from other animals, certainly in degree if not in uniqueness, in that much of their play need not be displayed in physical behavior but can be enacted in the imagination. It is not implausible, then, to suppose that the pleasure we derive from monster-slaying tales (in which humans kill monsters by virtue of wit as well as physical strength) stems in part from the same mental systems that reward us for juvenile play.

The foregoing deals with the possible origins of monster-slaying tales. Boyer's insights, however, and the insights of anthropologists with similar perspectives, can also help illumine the persistence of such tales and their transmission across generations. Focusing on religious ideas Boyer (1994, 2001) argues that successful religious ideas, that is, those that are likely to be best remembered and transmitted across generations, are ideas that approach what he calls a "cognitive optimum." Such an optimum is a certain balance between intuitive and counterintuitive expectations. Expectations relate to a small number of panhuman ontological categories: Animal, Person, Artifact, Natural Object, and Plant. Accordance with intuitive ontological expectations tends to make an idea plausible and easy to learn. On the other hand, its violation of such expectations, its counterintuitivity, can render it attention-getting and memorable. There are, however, constraints on what people are likely to accept and pass on, for not everything goes.

An idea that fully conforms to our intuitive ontological expectations tends to be uninteresting and thus a poor candidate for transmission. And one that severely departs from expectations grounded in intuitive ontologies is also a poor candidate for it is likely to be deficient in ideational support and lacks the inferential potential that could facilitate its "enrichment"—that is, its elaboration from cultural and personal archives of established ideas and expectations. Finally, violation of ontological expectations should not be confused with what is merely unusual for the instantiations of a category. Thus, for instance, while Dracula's great strength exceeds what is usual for entities pertaining to the Person category, it is not an ontological violation, since we normally expect some persons to be stronger than others, whereas Dracula's transformation into a nonhuman animal clearly is a violation.

We can apply Boyer's insights to folkloric monsters. They are often credited, for example, with Person-like will and cunning while departing in attention-getting ways from other category-related expectations. Two of their most arresting features, as noted earlier, are predation and boundary-transgressing hybridism. The former may or may not violate ontological assumptions about the Person category whereas the latter always does.

Predation involves death, which converts a human into a non-person. This in itself does not constitute a counterintuitive feature of the monster, but if the monster's agency reanimates the person whom the monster killed, as happens in many vampire stories where victims are turned into vampires, then the monster is counterintuitive on that score, for that kind of power is not part of our prototypical conceptualizations of the Person category. Hybridism contravenes essentialist notions to the effect that there are distinct, perdurable natures for all species, and it contravenes ancillary classificatory expectations about mutually exclusive categories.²

In the theorizing of cognitive scientists of various disciplinary affiliations, our evolved brain architecture predisposes us toward certain sorts of concept formations and works against or constrains possible others. Further, there are additional selective advantages (such as approaching Boyer's "cognitive optimum") enjoyed by some concepts as contrasted to others in cultural transmissions both within and between generations. The thrust of this theorizing suggests that there are natural resemblances, and not merely cultural resemblances, among humankind's many representations of monsters. This would help us to understand why we find recapitulations in various guises of monster-slaying motifs in cultures unconnected by time or place. And one such guise, we hold, is the prototypical vampire story found in Bram Stoker's *Dracula*.

6

Toward a Realistic and Relevant "Science of Religion"

Introduction

In approaching the country that some call "the science of religion," I feel obliged to identify myself as a sympathetic alien. In light of certain of my research interests, moreover, I hasten to add that I am fully terrestrial. But my passport is from an anthropology department rather than from a department of religion.

While anthropologists sometimes use the expression "science of religion," it is my impression that we more commonly talk about "the anthropology of religion." In doing so, some of us identify ourselves as anthropologists with special interests in nutrition, law, economics, and so forth.

In addition to resembling members of departments of religion by virtue of mutual interests in scholarly explorations of religion, anthropologists of religion overlap with them in another way. That is, members of both sorts of departments in the modern, secular academy recognize an obligation to bracket judgments about the truth-values of magico-religious claims (Wiebe

1999, 1990).[1] In practice, however, scholars in both groups sometimes resist or reject bracketing. Thus, for example, Evans-Pritchard relates much of his analysis in *Witchcraft, Oracles and Magic among the Azande* (1937) to his explicitly declared assumption that magic as such is false. And in his famous work, *The Meaning and End of Religion* (1962), Wilfred Cantwell Smith emphasizes what he calls the "impingement" of the Transcendent in human life, doubtlessly aware that for many of his readers impingement implies an impinge.

In any case, members of departments of religion and members of anthropology departments have engaged in lively debates in recent years about the nature, limitations, and possibilities of the scholarly study of religion. Both, indeed, have argued about whether or not their respective scholarly pursuits can be "science" in any acceptable, substantive sense of that term.

In the past (and even to some extent today) such debates sometimes touched on considerations of "autonomy." But when they did, they tended to do so with this difference: numbers of anthropologists argued about whether or not *culture* may be said to be autonomous, while members of departments of religion raised a parallel argument about *religion*—a parallel argument, but, of course, a different argument. Among themselves, anthropologists did not usually engage in debates about the possible "autonomy" of religion because many of them deemed religion to be a sort of department or subdivision of culture. But some members of departments of religion, at least in Canada and the United States, explicitly raised the issue of autonomy of religion. And, typically, advocates of a science of religion argued *against* the idea of autonomy. They sometimes did so in open opposition to those of their own academic colleagues who maintained that religion pivots on something that is irreducibly religious.

While agreeing with those scholars in departments of religion who argue against the idea that religion is autonomous or "*sui generis*," and while sympathetic to their desire to develop and sustain a science of religion, I have some reservations about the accomplishments of some (but not all) of them to date. My reservations also apply to the publications of many (but not all) anthropologists who study religion.

First, in my opinion, the outputs of both sorts of scholars of religion have not been as *relevant* to the findings of the sciences as they might have been (albeit I see signs of genuine—indeed, major—improvement in recent years). Second, and closely related to the matter of relevance, numbers of scholars of religion, both anthropologists and others, have not always been as *realistic* as they might have been. I turn now to considerations of what I mean by being realistic and relevant.

Being Relevant

I begin with relevance. At the very outset of my remarks about it, I acknowledge the clear relevance of the academic study of religion to both the goals and much of the substance of liberal arts curricula in European and North American universities. Religion has played a diversity of significant roles in much of human history. And, despite the predictions of the secularization hypothesis of some decades ago, religion continues to flourish. For these reasons, historical and comparative studies of religion are important not only for humanist scholars within the academy, but also for people outside of it who reflect seriously on the human condition. It is fitting, therefore, that the academy should recognize the significance of religion in human life by sheltering the study of it. But I am talking about the traditional locus of such study in the humanities. What of the call for a "science of religion"?

It seems to me that Donald Wiebe and numbers of others among our contemporaries express relatively modest views when they champion a "science of religion." Basically, they advocate four things.

First, they demand that the study of religion in secular universities be emancipated from the theological advocacies or other insinuations of positive religious biases. Some go further in that they require that the scientific study of religion be unencumbered by social and political involvements. As Wiebe put it at the 1997 Åbo Symposium on Methodology in the Study of Religions:

> [T]he task of the scientific student of religion is not a moral or social one; it is merely to describe and explain as comprehensively as possible the phenomenon of religious behavior. If we are to avoid the decomposition of the academic study of religion into a pseudo-science we must leave broader Religious Studies—with its political and social agendas—to the humanists and religious devotees concerned with their place as public intellectuals in the life of society.
>
> (Wiebe 1999:260–1)

Second, proponents of the scientific study of religion advocate that some of the perspectives of scientists and philosophers of science, and certain of their standards or recommendations for doing scientific research, be adopted as guidelines by scholars of religion.

Third, they incline to the view that the science of religion can seek in some sense to explain religious phenomena as distinct from "interpreting" such phenomena.

Finally, and in consonance with the first three points, some proponents of a science of religion recommend that the scientific study of religion be deemed a social science. As a social science, it will have its own subject matter, but it will invoke relevant psychological and sociological theories and constructs whenever it seems productive to do so.

While I think that some ambitions constitute steps in the right direction, I judge them to be inadequate. I do so because in social sciences such as cultural anthropology and sociology the dominant traditional model guiding research is defective.[2] Among other things, it does not emphatically and consistently encourage students of religion to connect their findings and theorizing to the findings and theorizing of other sciences, particularly the biological and cognitive sciences.

Here and there, to be sure, we encounter statements as one offered by Wiebe at Åbo: that, as he puts it, "[w]e need ... to establish more appropriate relations between our research and that of other established scientific fields" (1999:267). Wiebe, moreover, concludes his paper with what I deem a welcome suggestion: that "we need to reconsider the value of a return to evolutionary theory to re-establish a unifying framework for the study of religion" (1999:269). Yet although I agree with his remarks, I wonder about their context. Wiebe and like-minded others seem to be advocating the creation of yet another discipline within the framework of the existing social sciences. They remind me to some extent of those of the elders of Israel who demanded of the prophet Samuel, "make us a king to judge us like all the nations" (*First Samuel* 8). The "nations" that Wiebe and his cohort would join, however, have recently been subjected to some adverse judgments.

I refer to criticisms made of the social sciences in general by John Tooby, an anthropologist, and Leda Cosmides, a psychologist, in a jointly authored, long essay entitled "The Psychological Foundations of Culture" (1992). I deem those criticisms to be cogent and arresting. I think, moreover, that they apply to what seems to be envisioned by some proponents—and *de facto* practitioners—of a science of religion (as well as applying to legions of anthropologists engaged in the anthropology of religion). They do not apply, however, to the theorizing of those students of religion who affiliate themselves with the contemporary cognitive and evolutionary sciences. Some of these, in my opinion, have already taken important steps in the creation of a truly exciting science of religion (I shall say more on this later).

Tooby and Cosmides are judicious in their examination of what they call "the Standard Social Science Model." They find elements of truth in it. They acknowledge, moreover, that the model would not have been as influential as it is if it didn't impress many persons as being plausible and anchored in reality (1992:33). At the same time, however, they think that it suffers from some major defects. In consequence of those defects, they argue, the Standard Social Science Model seems to make the social sciences autonomous from the rest of science (1992:33). Such apparent isolation, they opine, is regrettable, and emancipation from the traditional model would be a positive good. They recommend efforts to replace the Standard Social Science Model with what they and Jerome Barkow call "integrated theory." An integrated theory, as they and Barkow describe it, is "one framed so that it is compatible with data and theory from other relevant fields" (Cosmides, Tooby, and Barkow 1992:4).

The Standard Social Science Model

What is "the Standard Social Science Model"? As Tooby and Cosmides characterize it, it is founded on, and seeks to deal with, observations of cultural and behavioral similarities *within* human groups and observations of cultural and behavioral differences *between* human groups. Contemporary social scientists correctly maintain that neither cultural similarities nor cultural differences can be explained by discrete and variable racial or genetic factors in human populations. All normal human infants everywhere enjoy much the same biological endowment, an endowment that makes possible a human level of existence. And biological factors as such do not determine which particular language people will speak or which particular culture they participate in.

Unfortunately, Tooby and Cosmides aver, while social scientists correctly maintain that the common biological endowment of normal human infants is everywhere much the same, many of them impose erroneous suppositions on that understanding. They hold that "human nature" is a constant, and a constant cannot explain a variable, the observed diversity of cultures. As the young of the human species develop, social scientists generally suppose, they must acquire what leads to differences among them. They must acquire it, that is, from extra-genetic, extra-somatic sources: from sociocultural, not biological, sources. In the Standard Social Science Model, sociocultural factors in effect create the individual and largely determine adult mental organization, with little or no input from biological variables.

The social scientists who argue this way usually acknowledge that "human nature"—which Tooby and Cosmides identify as "the evolved architecture of the human mind" (1992:28)—is a necessary condition for the cultural organization of human life. But they otherwise deny significant causal powers to it in accounting for cultural diversity. Many agree with Émile Durkheim's assertion that human nature is "merely the indeterminate material that the social factor molds and transforms" (quoted by Tooby and Cosmides 1992:28). Or, adopting a more contemporary idiom, they suppose, as does Clifford Geertz (1973:35), that the human mind is a sort of general purpose computer that requires the downloading of cultural programs if it is to operate in a discernibly human way. And, in something of a parallel to Mircea Eliade, the anthropologist Robert Lowie stoutly proclaims that "[c]ulture is a thing *sui generis* which can be explained only in terms of itself ... *Omnis cultura ex cultura*" (quoted in Tooby and Cosmides 1992:28).

The Standard Social Science Model, Tooby and Cosmides (1992:28) point out, "removes from the concept of human nature all substantive content, and relegates the architecture of the human mind to the delimited role of embodying 'the capacity for culture.'" Even emotions such as sexual jealousy or paternal love, they note, are accounted to be cultural products.

This viewpoint has nurtured all sorts of ancillary ideas, including, among others, both assumptions that problematics relate to the specifics of culture and the ways in which it is transmitted from generation to generation. It nurtures, for example, the assignment of importance to learning theory in psychology (with a concomitant relative neglect of other topical concerns in that discipline), the notion that the mind-brain is a general purpose processor (rather than an assemblage of domain-specific modules), and the preprocessing idea that the evolution of our capacity for culture has endowed our species with an enormous potentiality for behavioral flexibility, a flexibility that is ultimately constrained by culture itself.

Tooby and Cosmides call our attention to some specific defects in the Standard Social Science Model. For one thing, they write, its central logic rests on naive and erroneous concepts drawn from outmoded theories of development. For example, the fact that some aspect of adult mental organization is absent at birth has no bearing on whether it is part of our evolved architecture. Just as teeth or breasts are absent at birth, and yet appear through maturation, evolved psychological mechanisms or modules (complex structures that are functionally organized for processing) could develop at any point in the life cycle. For this reason, the many features of adult mental organization absent at birth need not be attributed to exposure to transmitted culture but may come about through a large number of causal avenues not considered in traditional analyses (1992:33).

For another thing, Tooby and Cosmides maintain, the Standard Social Science Model "rests on a faulty analysis of nature-nurture issues, stemming from a failure to appreciate the role that the evolutionary process plays in organizing the relationship between our species-universal genetic endowment, our evolved developmental processes, and the recurring features of developmental environments" (1992:33). They go on to say that the critique of the standard model "that has been emerging from the cognitive and evolutionary communities" is not simply the charge that proponents of that model have underestimated the importance of biological factors in human life. Rather, the target of criticism "is the whole framework that assumes the 'biological factors' and 'environmental factors' refer to mutually exclusive sets of causes that exist in some kind of explanatory zero-sum relationship" (1992:33).

Perhaps an even more devastating criticism is this: "The Standard Social Science Model," Tooby and Cosmides write, requires an *impossible* psychology. Results out of cognitive psychology, evolutionary biology, artificial intelligence, developmental psychology, linguistics, and philosophy converge on the same conclusion: A psychological architecture that consisted of nothing but equipotential, general-purpose, or content-free mechanisms *could not successfully perform* the tasks the human mind is known to perform or solve ... from seeing, to learning a language, to recognizing an emotional expression, to selecting a mate, to the many disparate activities aggregated under the term "learning culture" ... *It cannot account for the behavior observed, and* [in light of our understandings of the *ad hoc*, opportunistic nature of natural selection] *it is not a type of design that could have evolved.*

(1992:34, emphases added)

Without going any further into the particulars of the criticisms voiced by Tooby and Cosmides, suffice it to say that there is enough wrong with the Standard Social Science Model as to render it a dubious model for the science of religion. Its celebration of the imputed autonomy and power of culture nurtures close-ended hermeneutical and/or functionalist studies that have little or no cumulative payoff. As a paradigm for research and theorizing, moreover, the Standard Social Science Model serves to isolate many social scientists from exciting developments in contemporary philosophy, the cognitive sciences and linguistics, the neural sciences, evolutionary biology, and the development and evolutionary psychology. Indeed, the business-as-usual and almost exclusive emphasis on culture, ironically enough, works to inhibit the emergence of balanced and warrantable understandings of culture. As the anthropologist Roy D'Andrade (1995:216) puts it,

Many anthropologists believe culture does just about everything. ... But culture does not really do *everything*. The effect of culture is greatly exaggerated by many anthropologists. So far as we know, no cultural particulars are needed for humans everywhere to do *modus ponens,* or remember the color of apples, or perceive that a hawk is different than a handsaw.

A major, promising alternative view to that championed by the Standard Social Science Model is characterized in these words by Tooby and Cosmides (1992:34):

> [H]uman psychological architecture contains many evolved mechanisms that are specialized for solving evolutionarily long-enduring adaptive problems and ... these mechanisms have content-specialized representational formats, procedures, cues, and so on. These richly content-sensitive evolved mechanisms tend to impose certain types of content and conceptual organization on human mental life and, hence, strongly shape the nature of human social life and what is transmitted across generations.

Toward Relevance

How may the science of religion position itself with respect to the promises of that alternative view? How, indeed, may it render its research and theorizing *compatible with,* and *complementary to,* the research and theorizing of other sciences concerned with the human condition and, by so doing, make itself more *relevant* to those sciences? I think that there are a number of things that it can and should do. I limit myself here to advocating three of them.

First, the science of religion ought to be clear about the phenomenal subjects of its research. Those subjects, in my opinion, are not religions or cultures. Rather, they are human beings. Religion and culture are constructs that we associated with human beings. The emerging science of religion already views religion as a human creation, and we need to expand our knowledge of human being if we are to expand our knowledge of why and how they go about creating religions. To borrow an insight from theologians, a global perspective on creatures requires some understanding of their creator.

Second, the science of religion is out to address the most interesting and important questions that we can ask about religion, namely what should we mean by "religion?" Why are there religions? How are they organized and transmitted? In what ways do religions resemble one another and in what ways do they differ? And why do many people continue to invest themselves in religion whereas others distance themselves from it or actively attempt to debunk it?

Third, and in consonance with the above recommendations, the science of religion should be explicitly affiliated with the cognitive and evolutionary sciences. This does not mean that it would exclude descriptive or experimental studies that are outside of self-consciously cognitive and/or evolutionary frames. Descriptions, however, are observations that have been selected, organized, and reworked, and as such they are inevitably theory-laden. As Popper (1962) cogently argues, observations are perceptions that have been prepared by biases or, broadly put, by theories. Experiments, moreover, are normally organized to test hypotheses, and they are thus exercises in the service of theories. What I advocate, therefore, is that the dominant questions that frame the science of religion, and the methodological and theoretical weightings that identify it, be relevant to, informed by, and contributory to, work in the contemporary cognitive and evolutionary sciences.

The Cognitive Approach

Eschewing "superorganic" cultures, disembodied "social facts," and suprapersonal "structures" of appropriateness, contemporary cognitive studies take human beings as their phenomenal subjects, especially as they credit those subjects with mind-brains. Religion, in a manner of speaking, bubbles up from the mind-brain.

Many (perhaps most) contemporary students of religion who espouse cognitive approaches endorse what has come to be known as the modular theory of mind (Hirschfeld and Gelman 1994). That is, the mind-brain is envisioned as including a number of different "modules" or "intelligences." These are evolved and varied mental structures that are sensitive, respectively, to different sorts of inputs that stem from our perceptual machinery and/or the outputs of other modules. They are disposed, moreover, to process information in determinate ways. It is hypothesized, for example, that while some module(s) may be engaged mainly with language disposition and acquisition, others are primarily involved with mathematical skills, or agent detection, or hazard avoidance, and so on.

Our conceptual inferential systems, in this view, are modularly funded, and as such not everything goes. The mind-brain is not content-free, and our concepts and inferences are disposed in certain ways, regardless of our culture. The mind-brain, moreover, is not unconstrained, and neither are our concepts and inferences. Since religion relates to our conceptual and inferential propensities, we do not find in actuality certain imaginable kinds of religion (Boyer 1994, 2001), just as language users do not normally make certain imaginable kinds of syntactical errors.

We humans, cognitive students of religion maintain, enjoy a number of capacities, dispositions, and processing capabilities that originally had, and that still have, adaptive significance. Thus, by way of three examples: we have agent-detection sensitivities (useful not only in social relations with conspecifics but also in monitoring the world for real and imagined opportunities and dangers); we can imagine virtual realities (which allow us both to envision future what-if scenarios and to account in one way or another for the past); and we have metarepresentational abilities that we employ in attempting to understand and predict the behavior of others.

Such capacities, propensities, and processual capabilities, as Boyer (2004) argues, would be with us regardless of whether or not we have religion. They underwrite multiple domains of human life and religion is among their derivatives. Thus, by way of a very brief (and simplified) effort at illustration, our agent-detector sensitivities, coupled with our capacities and dispositions to imagine virtual realities, may lead us to infer and conceptualize nonexistent beings of the sort that students of religion call gods. And our metarepresentational capacities and propensities may support the attribution of will, desire, and purpose to those imagined gods by persons who deem them real.

Acknowledgment of the derivative nature of religion raises problems for the explanation of religion. It cannot suffice either to rely on religious people for sufficient leads or to rely on the constructs of armchair theorists. Cogent and persuasive explanations of religion must depend on bringing to light the mental structures that underwrite religion and much else in human life, and it is unlikely that questioning religious people or closely reading the classical literature will do that adequately. That is why numbers of cognitive students of religion have designed and executed various experiments, as well as accessing the already established experimental literature in psychology. Not all experimenters, by the way, are psychologists. Anthropologists such as Scott Atran and Pascal Boyer, and humanists-turned-scientists such as Ilkka Pyysiäinen, have resorted to experiments in order to test hypotheses and so better understand why we have religion. This does not mean that future fieldwork, or survey research, or textual analysis, or many other traditional avenues of scholarship are to be ruled out. It does mean, however, that a truly scientific study of religion is unashamedly reductive (Boyer 2004), and that it will make sense of the fruits of other research by relating them to cognitive (and perhaps eventually neural) processes.

Evolution

Our descriptive and experimental studies could benefit by relating to evolutionary theory for at least two reasons. First, since religions are human creations, our understanding of them (as I suggested earlier) will be advanced by a greater knowledge of their creators, and a global understanding and appreciation of the human condition requires a phylogenetic perspective (Hallowell 1960). Second, Darwinian (or, if you prefer, neo-Darwinian) theory is supported by a great deal of empirical evidence, it is underwritten by sound logic, and it is powerful in that it is used to explain much.

Now, evolutionary interests were in evidence among some nineteenth-century students of religion. Their ways of addressing and expressing those interests, however, eventually displeased later students of religions. Evans-Pritchard (1965), for example, dismissed Edward Burnett Tylor's intellectualist and evolutionary theorizing as summing to a "Just-So" story.

Today, however, we are in a better position to support an evolutionary perspective and shelter the science of religion under it. We benefit from a much more sophisticated understanding of evolution than that enjoyed by our nineteenth-century predecessors. This better understanding rests on a host of developments. They include (but are not limited to) the creation of new disciplines such as genetics and molecular biology and the flourishing of organic chemistry, paleontology, and evolutionary biology; advances in the cognitive and neural sciences; the development of increasingly sophisticated mathematical and statistical techniques (as in population genetics and in numbers of other fields); the use of electronic computers for handling large amounts of data; new discoveries in paleoanthropology and the rise and promise of cognitive archaeology; and, after some mixed reviews for sociobiology, the florescence of evolutionary psychology.

Perhaps the most important evolutionary question a student of religion may ask is this: Did religion evolve? No, Scott Atran (2002) answers, because there neither is nor was an "it" to have evolved. Religion, as I (Saler 1994, 1997, 1999, 2000a [1993], 2000b) argue in a nonessentialist vein, is a variable congeries of different elements and not some specific this or that. The elements that we associate with religion did not evolve together; rather, they arose as spandrels in the evolution of certain capacities and dispositions that offered adaptive advantages. Religion, Boyer (2001, 2004) points out, is parasitic on different evolved adaptive capacities and propensities that, quite apart from religion, play important roles in sustaining human life.

Given the understandings outlined above, it follows that the evolutionary studies that are most immediately relevant to the science of religion are those that illumine, and that seek in some sense to account for, the emergence of the cognitive capacities and dispositions that support religion. But, as claimed above, such capacities and dispositions support religion. However, such capacities and dispositions support much else, and they did not originally merge because of their importance to religion. These views are fundamental to an important book published by the archeologist Steven Mithen (1996) and appropriately titled *The Prehistory of the Mind*. The encompassing nature of that study, already affirmed by the title, is reinforced by the subtitle: *The Cognitive Origins of Art, Religion and Science*.[3]

Mithen incorporates some of his findings into a later and more particularized paper entitled "Symbolism and the Supernatural" (1999), and it is worth citing here some of what he says in that essay by way of further supporting the recommendation that the science of religion incorporate an evolutionary dimension.

"Symbolism and the Supernatural"

Mithen holds that ideas about the supernatural can be anchored in the mind with the help of material artifacts, and that without such anchorage religious institutions and thought about the supernatural would be severely constrained (1999:148). Archeologists, of course, are professionally motivated and trained to unearth and analyze material artifacts and so, among other things, to look for material symbols that might promote religious conceptualizations (1999:50).

In surveying the archeological record both in the 1996 book and in the later paper, Mithen comes to conclusions that some may regard as surprising.

Contrary to the supposition that religious thought is ancient in our *genus*, Mithen claims that "the archeological evidence suggests that religious ideas and ritual activities appeared relatively recently in human prehistory" (1999:151). While archaic members of the *genus* Homo appeared in the fossil record 2.5 million years ago, our first unambiguous (albeit slight) evidence for religious rituals is not more than 100,000 years old (1999:151). That evidence comes from burials where animal remains were interred with human dead. But evidence of *manufactured or artificially made symbols* suggest that religion is no earlier than perhaps 30,000 years ago (1999:151).

Mithen thinks it likely that religious beliefs arose as "mental spandrels," that is, as originally non-adaptive by-products of other, adaptive cognitive developments (1999:157). He hypothesizes a "protosymbolism" among our ancestors in the Upper Paleolithic (1999:153-4). Prior to some 60,000 to 30,000 years ago, he conjectures, early human ancestors had at least three specialized cognitive domains, to wit, intelligences concerned with material objects, with living entities, and with the human social world. While each of these domains may have facilitated discrete or specialized complexities (such as Neanderthal skills in producing Levallois flakes and points) (1999:158), early humans did not connect skills facilitated by one domain with skills facilitated by other domains (1999:159). Mithen thinks it likely that that was because "their thoughts about the social, natural, and technical worlds were quite isolated from each other" (1999:159).

Eventually, however, Mithen suggests, there was a transition to what he calls "cognitive fluidity" (1999:159), where the different domains penetrated and supported one another. That transition was of immense evolutionary significance. The integration of the three kinds of intelligence facilitated not only the design of new hunting weapons, but also the production of artifacts such as beads and necklaces that conveyed social messages (1999:159). Mithen supposes *Homo sapiens sapiens* to have attained greater "cognitive fluidity" than Neanderthals and that that achievement was a major factor in accounting for the replacement of the latter by the former.

Mithen applies these claims to the development of religious ideas and their expression and anchorage in material artifacts. Drawing upon Pascal Boyer's (1994) emphasis on the distinction between intuitive and counterintuitive ontologies, and Stewart Guthrie's (1993) treatment of anthropomorphism, Mithen suggests that cognitive fluidity makes possible the combining of the intuitive and the counterintuitive and the anthropomorphizing of animals by attributing to them human-like intelligence, will, and purpose. Such combinations and attribution, he argues, need not have any adaptive value. Indeed, these and other religious ideas can be non-adaptive or even maladaptive. But whatever their possible cost, that cost is "more than compensated for by the benefits of cognitive fluidity gained from other types of thinking" (1999:160).

Now, Mithen's thesis has a certain plausibility to it. And, when evaluated against the artifactual evidence for it, it is a brilliant demonstration of how archeologists can sometimes make much out of relatively little. While decidedly speculative, it does, however, have three things in its favor. First, it takes account of the actual material evidence available. That evidence clearly confronts us with puzzles. Artifacts thus far unearthed indicate that for hundreds of thousands of years our early tool-making ancestors were decidedly "conservative," turning out much the same crude tools year after year. Then, rather suddenly, there was a florescence of new types of tools and, necessarily, new techniques for producing them. Why? Mithen supposes that something in the nature of a cognitive revolution must have occurred. Second, Mithen takes account of a large and diverse literature on the nature of the mind and he selectively and adroitly applies that literature to solving some archeological puzzles. Third, he attempts to account for the emergence of religion by relating it both to the material evidence in hand and to some powerful theories of religion offered by contemporary cognitive students of religion. In my opinion, Mithen deserves our admiration on all three counts, even if does not fully persuade us.

Now, at first glance, Mithen's approach may seem to clash with that of one of my teachers, Anthony F. C. Wallace. I think, however, that those approaches can be productively related to one another and that both should be taken into account by the science of religion.

Anthony F. C. Wallace

Wallace was fond of telling his students that if they were to seek the origins of religion, they should look not to the Paleolithic but to their daily newspapers. That is because, he continued, religion originates again and again in human history. Because it does, he held, it becomes possible through ethnographic, historical, and comparative research to identify the typical conditions under which religions emerge. We can hope, indeed, to develop a model of religion's usual patterns of emergence and development and to hypothesize relevant explanatory mechanisms that might account for components of the model. In consonance with those convictions, as some of you may know, Wallace (1956b) offers us his model of "revitalization movements." Drawing, moreover, on Pavlov's work on ultraparadoxical reactions, on Selye's work on stress at "The General Adaptation Syndrome," and on much else, he adumbrates the mechanism of "mazeway resynthesis." Wallace's major paper on mazeway resynthesis (1956a), be it noted, is subtitled "A Biocultural theory of Religious Inspiration."

Wallace more or less assumes the existence of the cognitive capacities and propensities the emergence of which Mithen seeks to trace in the archeological record. That is why I think the difference approaches of these two scholars are sequentially compatible. There is, moreover, a larger lesson to be drawn from that compatibility. Part of the work of the science of religion, in tandem with other sciences, is to understand the emergence and nature of the cognitive capacities that underwrite religion. And in illuminating the possibilities and limitations of those capacities, we provide other scholars with powerful tools for better understanding the careers of religions mentioned in their daily newspapers.

Being Realistic

I have devoted much of this essay to sketching some of my views on the matter of relevance. Now I turn to the related challenge of rendering the science of religion more realistic. I do not employ "realistic" in any formal philosophical sense. Rather, I use it in its common and idealized acceptations: that is, as having to do with accommodations to facts and to good arguments, and a corresponding disinclination to accept the fanciful and the illogical. The place to start, I think, is with our understandings of language.

More particularly, we may start with a realistic appreciation of language's limitations. The most important of those limitations as they relate to the study of religion is language's lack of full transparency in communicating thought and in representing the world. There are several reasons for why that is the case. Thus, for instance, structural requirements internal to any system of signs constrain the arbitrariness of expressive vehicles if meaning combinations are to be predictable sign combinations; language, in consequence, cannot be internally cohesive as well as fully transparent to the meanings it expresses (Parmentier 1985:372). For another thing, we humans are prone to expand our understandings analogically, and analogical expansions motivate tropes. We must reckon with the fact that our uses render many of the terms that we employ polysemous (i.e., a given term takes on different meanings, though those meanings are systematically related to one another).[4] Terms, moreover, are likely to be loaded with connotations, and sensitivities (or insensitivities) to connotations may vary among members of a speech community. For these and other reasons, the goal of a tidy and strictly neutral scientific language would seem to be unrealistic, especially when it comes to the study of human affairs. The conceit that students of the human condition can systematically and consensually employ one term for one thing is not supportable, either historically or in principle.

What are we to do? We can endorse some realistic suggestions offered by the philosopher Karl Popper (1962). We should strive not for utter or exhaustive precision in specifying what may be meant by our analytical terms but for serviceable clarity in explicating how they are used.

In attempting to implement Popper's suggestion, some plain talk about categories and concepts can be useful. "Categorization," the psychologist Douglas Medin writes,

> involves treating two or more distinct entities as in some way equivalent in the service of accessing knowledge and making predictions ... a *concept* is an idea that includes all that is characteristically associated with it. A *category* is a partitioning or class to which some assertion or set of assertions might apply.
>
> (Medin 1989:1469, emphases in original)

Categories, in brief, are classificatory devices. As such, they relate to other categories, other classificatory devices, in larger classificatory structures. Categories, moreover, express and may be motivated by knowledge and theories about the world, including knowledge and theories about what counts as meaningful resemblances. Altering what we may mean by some category—religion, say—is therefore not as easy or as unconstrained as some may suppose although, of course, history teaches us that categories and larger classificatory structures do change.

Apposite to the subject matter of this essay is the category "religion." Numbers of students of religion have remarked on the contested nature of the category. Because some of them deem definitional issues to be crucial for marking out an area of study, I will center the rest of this essay on that subject. A realistic "science of religion," many will agree, requires a realistic explication of "religion."

A Few Examples of Approaches to the Definitional Problem

Many persons have sought to define religion by specifying putative "distinctive features,"[5] features represented to be both necessary and sufficient for identifying instances of the category (see Saler 2000a [1993]: 87–157 for criticisms of a diversity of example). A smaller number of authors have advocated an anti-essentialist "family resemblance" approach to defining religion, but some of them have subverted their own recommendations in ways that suggest essentialist recidivism (e.g., Peter Byrne 1988:7, 9; see Fitzgerald 1996: 227 and Saler 1999: 393–4 for some criticisms of Byrne).

Other scholars have advocated, for one reason or another, that we jettison the category and category label. W. C. Smith (1962), for example, recommends that we substitute "cumulative traditions" and "faith" for "religion." Timothy Fitzgerald (1996, 1997, 2000), penning an even more radical set of suggestions, would have us do away not only with the category but also with departments of religion or religious studies as presently constituted; he advocates that such departments be converted into departments of cultural studies dedicated to the exploration of values and power realities.

A concern with "power" also animates much of Talal Asad's 1983 essay, "Anthropological Conceptions of Religion: Reflections on Geertz," an essay well received by a number of anthropologists. Asad does not advocate that we do away with the term and category "religion." But because of an unfortunate incoherence in his argument, he in effect turns the category into one that might more appropriately be labeled "*je ne sais quoi*." Asad maintains the following: (1) Clifford Geertz's famous 1966 characterization of religion, one that emphasizes meaning and general order, is a privatized, "Christian" conception of religion and is unsuitable as a cross-cultural analytical category. (2) Many anthropologists have operated with similar conceptions of religion, and they would do well to purge themselves of such conceptions in light of the criticisms made of Geertz. (3) Instead of addressing the questions about meaning made of Geertz favored in 1966, students of religion should address the question: how does power create religion? Asad, however, fails to bridge a rather daunting gap between his first two points and the third. That is, if we truly purged our minds of Geertz-like conceptions of religion, conceptions that (allegedly) have hitherto guided us, don't we need some new conception if we are going to study how "power" creates "religion?" Asad, alas, fails to supply anything in the way of a substitute. And so, in the end, he in effect recommends that we study how power creates *je ne sais quoi* (or something equivalently vacuous).

In that we have touched on considerations of "power," it seems relevant to consider an assertion that, if accepted at face value, would greatly empower scholars. I refer to a statement made by Jonathan Z. Smith: "'Religion' is not a native term; it is a term created by scholars for their intellectual purposes and therefore is theirs to define" (1998:281). While I do not accept that statement as it stands, it can be reduced to the making of a sustainable point: that scholars have some options in defining religion.

Scholars, however, are not the only people who talk about religion. Nor are they the only ones who sometimes raise questions about the meaning of the term. To restrict our purview to contemporary American society, there are, for example, the courts that interpret and generalize constitutional restrictions on the Congress respecting the establishment and prohibition of religion. And then there are various federal, state, and local agencies that require standard conceptions of religion for some of their routine work (e.g., in granting tax exemptions, adhering to zoning rules, and so forth). And, for that matter, there are also radio and television "talking heads," barbers and pastry chefs, mafia dons and copy editors, priests, ministers, rabbis, and imams, and all the other millions and millions of native or naturalized Americans who use the word "religion" and who occasionally venture explications of it. In actuality, while scholars have options when it comes to talking about religion, they are also constrained if they would communicate with one another and with a larger audience. And that's where being realistic could improve matters.

Some Realistic Considerations

Religion, the anthropologist Melford E. Spiro notes, "is a term with historically rooted meanings" (1966:91). Because of that, Spiro opines, "a definition must satisfy not only the criterion of cross-cultural applicability but also the criterion of intra-cultural intuitivity; at the last it should not be counter-intuitive" (1966:91).

Religion is indeed a term with "historically rooted meanings." And its history is decidedly complex. Furthermore, as numbers of scholars have noted, many non-Western populations lack traditional terms and categories that approximate to terms and categories for "religion" in the contemporary West. Euro-Americans, however, have exported—in some cases imposed—conceptions of religion, and vocabularies for talking about it, throughout the globe.

The emergence of modern Western conceptions of religion is related in multiplex ways to the Reformation and accompanying wars and persecutions, the influx of information from the New World and the desires of Europeans to classify and assimilate that information, the Enlightenment and the rise of deism, the developments of capitalism and colonialism, the florescence of secular scholarly studies, and still more.

Today, "religion" is a widely diffused popular term and category in Euro-American societies. Scholars have appropriated both, and numbers of them have sought to refine, reform, or reinvent the category (only a minority, insofar as I am aware, express themselves in favor of doing away with it). Efforts at scholarly refinement, reform, or reinvention often involve some distancing from popular uses, but largely in attempts to foreground what, in the variegated opinions of scholars, may be most noteworthy, salient, or important about religion. Scholarly interests in religion, nevertheless, relate in great measure to the fact that religion has been, and remains, a matter of interest and concern in Euro-American societies.

However distanced scholarly applications of the term "religion" may become from popular applications, it is unlikely that they will break entirely with them. Maintaining universes of discourse is important not only within scholarly communities but also between such communities and the larger societies that support them. And here is where one of the major problems in religious studies lies.

Prototypical Exemplars

As I suggest elsewhere (Saler 2000a [1993]), for many Euro-Americans, those large families of religion that are popularly denominated "Judaism" and "Christianity" constitute *the most prototypical exemplars* of religion. I employ "prototype" in the sense described by the psychologist Eleanor Rosch (1978:36): "By prototypes of categories, we have generally meant the clearest cases of category membership defined operationally by people's judgements of goodness of membership in the category."[6] The judgment that "Judaism" and "Christianity" are prototypical poses a serious but not insurmountable problem for the prescription of a scholarly analytical category.

"Judaism" and "Christianity" constitute peculiar developments when compared, say, to traditional religions in highland New Guinea or lowland South America. They have published canons, articulated creeds, and accreted theological literatures, for example, and these were facilitated by a host of distinct economic, organizational, and technological developments. Many contributors to the developing theologies of those religions, moreover, found stimulation, positive and negative, in intellectual traditions originating outside of distinctly Jewish or Christian religious frames (e.g., in the panoplies of classical Greek and Hellenistic thought).

Coming to understand religion on the basis of cases that many Euro-Americans deem the most prototypical exemplars of the category can have—and has had—some unfortunate consequences (I furnish an example from lowland South American in Saler n.d.). As Pascal Boyer puts it,

> The focus on what we are familiar with—those highly doctrinal phenomena people call "world religions"—is the source of many a confused view about religion. For instance, it is in my experience exceedingly difficult to convince most people … that most religion is not about the creation of the world, that it is rarely about God, that it is very seldom about the salvation of the soul. More important and more difficult to impress upon most people: most religion has no doctrine, no set catalogue of beliefs that most members should adhere to, nor overall integrated statements about supernatural agents. Most religion is piecemeal, mostly implicit, often less than perfectly consistent and, most importantly, *focused on concrete circumstances.*
>
> (Boyer 2004:28, emphasis in original)

"Doctrinal" or so-called world or organized religions, Boyer (2004:29) argues, do not *displace* non-doctrinal religions but *supplement* them. They manifest an "additional growth." As such, they constitute "a secondary, derivative development of a much more general and deeply human tendency to imagine important supernatural agents and to entertain precise descriptions of their powers" (2004:28). One must understand this "general mental disposition," Boyer maintains, in order to understand much about "the special case" of religion as exemplified by so-called world religions (2004:28). Yet many students of religion, Boyer notes, have used doctrinal religions as a starting point in the attempt "to climb all the way up to a general understanding of religion in human kind," and doing so "was not always very successful" (2004:28).

I agree with much of what Boyer says in the citations given above. I wish, however, that he had expressed himself differently when we suggest that because the foregoing is the case,

> the dull business of demarcating what is "religion" from what is not is better left to lexicographers; it should not unduly trouble scholars. Whether accounts of religion are of interest depends, not on where they place its boundaries but on how they account for the observed behavior they purport to explain.
>
> (Boyer 2004:27)

Boyer is clearly operating with a concept of religion. Elsewhere, indeed, he tells us much about it (e.g., Boyer 2001). In the passage quoted, however, he appears to slight interest in specifying (and justifying) that concept in favor of emphasizing the importance of good explanation.

Inasmuch as this essay is concerned with developing a science of religion, I will outline what I prefer to mean by "religion." Before doing so, however, it may prove useful to take another look at "doctrinal" religion as a starting place for coming to understand religion. Such a starting place, it should be noted, can be problematic not only for understanding "traditional" religions, but also for understanding what occurs among the adherents of doctrinal religions. Many Christians, for example, are not very knowledgeable about Christian doctrines as described in textbooks or theological tracts. Or, even when knowledgeable, some reject various doctrines. Numbers of them, indeed, evince ideas, norms, and behaviors that are given little or no public endorsement by "mainstream" Christian theologians and church leaders.

Many field anthropologists, nevertheless, identify what they take to be religion in non-Western societies by finding analogies to what they deem to be "religion" at home. Given our intellectual propensities to assimilate new information, at least initially, by relating it to established representations and theories, that is hardly surprising. While this can sometimes conduce to errors, I do not think that it always does. Intelligence and hard work—and enough time in the field to maximize their possibilities—have often overcome initial bias. We can now, moreover, enhance prospects for realistic descriptions of religions by instituting safeguards derived from cognitive approaches. One very important safeguard is the recognition that "doctrinal" religions do not displace or obviate more general and widespread religious proclivities, even among declared adherents of "doctrinal" religions. Another is the understanding that because "doctrinal" religions show us what may become of more general religion under certain circumstances, they have to be selectively discounted as templates in the study of other religions.

Categories and Categorization

A science of religion, in my opinion, needs to consider what psychologists, philosophers, linguists, and others have learned and proposed about categories and categorization. That is, we need to consider such matters as they apply to us as analysts, in addition to considering what they may purport for the people we study. One might, for example, expand on what Coleman and Kay (1981: 27) describe as "the obvious pretheoretical intuition that semantic categories frequently have blurry edges and allow degrees of membership." And one might also explore Wittgenstein's insight: that, as Rosch (1978:36) describes it, "we can judge how clear a case something is and deal with categories on the basis of clear cases in the total absence of information about boundaries."

In an old and idealized approach to categorization, the members of a group comprehended by a category—the instantiations of the category—are viewed as fully and equally members by virtue of sharing in common one or more "distinctive features." Those features define the category and serve as standards for admission. This understanding works in the case of some categories (e.g., "triangle"). It is unsatisfactory, however, where some of the instances labeled by a term appear to have little or nothing in common with some of the other instances labeled by the same term. In the case of "game," for instance, what distinctive features does solitaire share with baseball? In this case, the philosopher Wittgenstein advises,

> Don't say: "There *must* be something common, or they would not be called 'games'"—but *look and see* whether there is anything common to all—For if you look at them you will not see something that is common to all, but similarities, relationships, and a whole series of them at that.
>
> (1958: I.66, emphasis in original)

Games, Wittgenstein says, "form a family" (*Philosophical Investigations* I.67), and they are linked together by "a complicated network of similarities overlapping and crisscrossing: sometimes overall similarities, sometimes similarities of detail" (1958: I.66). (Wittgenstein, by the way, did not invent the expression "family resemblances." It or similar expressions have long been in use in English, German, and other languages.)

"Game" constitutes a fairly extreme illustration because of the great diversity of games. In the particular examples that I have supplied, solitaire and baseball, there are no obvious similarities. Those examples, however, are linked together by networks of other games that resemble one or both. Thus bridge resembles solitaire in being a card game, and partnerships in bridge resemble to some extent the division into teams we find in baseball.

Wittgenstein maintains that *it is not necessary* for all the instantiations of a category to share features in common in order for them to be labeled by the same category term. He allows, however, that sometimes the instantiations of a category do share elements in common, albeit that sharing may not be of primary importance for understanding meaning.

Something of a parallel claim has been entered in an approach to summarizing the distribution of recognized features in a classification. I refer to "numerical phenetics" in biological systematics and its emphasis on so-called polythetic classification. The anthropologist Richard Chaney (1978:139–40) points out that while Wittgenstein's employment of the expression "family resemblance" has to do with "how we use our words and concepts," "polythetic classification," in contrast, is "actuarial data summary."

Both Wittgenstein and numerical pheneticists attempt, in their different ways and for different purposes, to comprehend phenomena in multi-factorial fashion. Wittgenstein, as noted earlier, allows that in some cases all of the instantiations of a category may share one or more features in common, but that even if they do that fact by itself may not disclose what is most significant about the category. Numerical pheneticists, for their part, allow that the members of a biological taxon are likely to share one or more "character states" in common (Sokal and Sneath 1963:14). But even though "natural taxa are usually not fully polythetic," for operational purposes pheneticists proceed as if they were (Sneath and Sokal 1973:21–2). Polythetic taxa, indeed, may revolve around monothetic cores.

Without going any further into technicalities,[7] suffice it to say that the two quite different intellectual engagements referred to above mutually support an important point. Briefly put, in anything as complex as biological systematics or the exploration of how we use terms and concepts in everyday life, we need to maximize the diversity of relevant variables and values taken into account. This is so even if we can identify one or more common features. In applying that insight to our interest in concepts and categories, it can be argued that we ought to consider a wealth of possibilities. That would include possible theories or "idealized cognitive models" that may help explain the structures of categories, the relevance of contexts for affecting conceptual strategies and tactics, variable weightings of features, and constraints on what people may be prepared to recognize (Lakoff 1987; Medin 1989). Rather than pursue this line of thought abstractly, however, I turn now to a limited discussion of a particular case: that of "supernatural agents" as we find them not only in what we unhesitatingly regard as "religion" but elsewhere as well.

Supernatural Agents

Boyer makes the postulation of supernatural agents central to his conceptualization of religion. Such agents conform for the most part to intuitive ontologies and expectations about persons as agents while departing from those ontologies and expectations in a relatively small number of arresting particulars (Boyer 1994, 2001). Supernatural agents, Boyer writes, are "defined as violations of intuitions about agents" (2004:31).[8] But as Boyer acknowledges on the same page, in addition to occurring in religion, "supernatural characters" are also "found in folktales and other minor cultural domains." I would go further. In our society, certainly, references to supernatural agents are widely encountered, if only as rhetorical ploys. Many such references are not usually taken as assertions of the reality of such agents (except, perhaps, as tropes). There are, however, references that do appear to implicate ontological commitments.

Supernatural agents are encountered in what we are likely to regard as the most prototypical (the adjudged "clearest") cases of religion. And they can be absent in some instances of what certain authors call "secular religions" or "quasi-religions," assemblages of elements that resemble more prototypical exemplars of religion, but not sufficiently enough to escape qualification. To complicate matters further, they are sometimes encountered in cases that many classify without explicit qualification as "religion" while deeming them somewhat ambiguous instances of that category. The canon of Canonical Theravada Buddhism, for example, recognizes gods but does not assign them salvific functions (salvation is realized only by following the teachings of the Buddha). Largely because it does not, both Durkheim

(1965 [1912]) and Southwold (1978) deny that theism is crucial to the definition of religion (Southwold argues that gods are contingent elements in religion, not necessary ones). But, as Spiro (1982 [1970]) points out, many Theravada Buddhists, despite what is inscribed in the canon, seek to invoke, propitiate, or avoid a variety of beings that he terms "superhuman." Spiro (1966) also argues that the Buddha is himself a "superhuman" being and therefore godlike, an argument that Southwold (1978) rejects as vague and unpersuasive.

Putting aside arguments about the Buddha, suffice it to suggest that the resolution of arguments about the status of gods and other supernatural agents in Theravada Buddhism ought to involve some functional considerations. Because the canon stresses salvation and accords no crucial or central importance to gods or other supernatural agents for obtaining it, we can argue that it does not render them religious objects.

Many Theravada Buddhists, however, in invoking or propitiating god-like beings in the hope of relieving sickness or enhancing prospects for success in various undertakings do treat them in a way that can induce us to classify them as religious objects.

Functional considerations also apply to other cases where (according to Boyer's characterization) we find supernatural agents but it would be stretching things to call them religious objects. Our allowance that this is so conduces, in my opinion, to at least three conclusions.

First, references to supernatural agents do not by themselves establish the existence of religion. While such references are *typical* of religion, they are certainly not *sufficient* for applying the category label. People, in my opinion, must deem supernatural agents to offer prospects of making significant differences in their lives if we are to account those agents religious objects. While postulations of supernatural agents can be numbers among religion-constituting elements, it is only when they are supported by other religion-constituting elements in appropriate contexts that we have religion.

Second, if we deem admission to a group comprehended by the category "religion" to be a matter of "more or less" rather than a matter of "yes or no," then an argument can be made for admitting "secular religions" and "quasi-religions" as peripheral members. Some of these peripheral cases, as indicated earlier, do not accord functional significance to supernatural agents or even call attention to them, unlike more central (more prototypical) exemplars of religion. If this be accepted, we could go on to argue that supernatural agents, though clearly typical of religion, are not *necessary* elements for recognizing religion.

Third, the wide occurrence of supernatural agents outside of what we unhesitatingly call religion is a matter of considerable interest. Boyer explains cogently *why* supernatural agents occur. But, despite some interesting things that he says in Boyer 2001, he does not broadly assess *the consequences* of their occurrences in diverse areas of human life. The developing science of religion may profitably do so. Indeed, by tracing the significance of elements that we deem typical of religion as they occur outside of the clear purview of what we conventionally call religion, we transcend religion. To the extent, that is, that we study elements that we regard as especially typical of religion in less typical settings, we attend to a *religious dimension* in human life that reaches out beyond religion.

Toward a Scholarly Model of Religion

A scholarly model of religion, as I conceive it, should consist of a pool of elements that scholars associate with religions. Not all will be found in all religions. Some will be more typical of what we mean by religion than others, both in terms of distributions and weightings. And many will be found outside of the purview of what scholars conventionally designate as religions. None by themselves are sufficient for doing so.

The approach outlined above emphasizes central tendencies rather than essences, fuzzy peripheries rather than sharp boundaries, resemblances rather than identities, and typical features rather than distinctive ones. Grounded in informed accommodations to the realities of language and categorization rather than in quixotic requirements for transparency and precision, and with relevance to the cognitive and evolutionary sciences, it encourages us both to explore religion and to transcend it. While religion and a religious dimension in human life are neither *sui generis* nor autonomous, and so not immune to reductive explanation, they are facets of the human conditions, and it makes analytical as well as existential sense to conceptualize them as such.

NOTES

Chapter 6

1. Some students of religion have gone well beyond minimalist commitments in that regard. Some have argued that magico-religious beliefs can only be properly understood within the context of the form of life that includes them, and were we to judge them true or false without such an understanding, we would be judging our own misunderstandings. Others have taken such a perspective even further.

   Maintaining that there are no transcendental, rational canons for truth and falsehood that apply universally, they hold that truth and falsehood are authorized by discourses. Since there are no universal standards, and since discourses differ, it would be meretricious, they suggest, to assert unequivocal, public judgments respecting the truth values of other people's magico-religious beliefs.

2. Some anthropologists and sociologists reject the idea that members of their disciplines should aspire to science. Instead of attempting to explain cultural phenomena, they hold, we should furnish "thick descriptions" and cogent interpretations. Others, however, call for theorizing that incorporates or emphasizes causality. I am concerned here with the dominant model that traditionally has guided the latter set of social scientists.

3. That subtitle is given on the title page of the paperback edition in my possession. The cover of that edition, however, does not include religion in the subtitle.

4. If the different meanings were not systematically related to one another, we would encounter homonomy, not polysemy.

5. I prefer the expression "distinguishing features" to the more commonly employed "distinctive features." The latter is more likely than the former to suggest characteristics or qualities that are independent of human judgments. "To distinguish," in contrast, implies the interposition of human agency in simultaneous acts of identifying and classifying.

6. A great deal of research has demonstrated that people often judge some instantiations of a category to be "clearer" or "better" exemplars than others. Thus, for example, some English speakers judge robins to be clearer exemplars of the category "bird" than penguins, and chair to be a better exemplar of "furniture" than radio. Disparities in judgments rendered have been called "prototype effects" (see, for example, Lakoff 1987).

7 More substantial descriptions and comparisons of polythesis and family resemblance can be found in Saler (2000a [1993]: chapter 5).

8 Defining *supernatural* agents as counterintuitive could go a long way toward resolving old arguments about the probity and utility of the term "supernatural." See Pyysiaäinen (2001).

BIBLIOGRAPHY

Aristotle. 1941. *The Basic Works of Aristotle*. Edited by Richard McKeon, Basic Books.
Asad, Talal. 1983. "Anthropological Conceptions of Religion: Reflections on Geertz." *Man*, vol. 18, no. 2, pp. 237–59.
Athanasius of Alexandria. 1996. *On the Incarnation: The Treatise of De Incarnatione Verbi Dei*. Edited and translated by A Religious of C.S.M.V. St Vladimir's Seminary Press.
Atran, Scott. 1990. *Cognitive Foundations of Natural History: Towards an Anthropology of Science*. Cambridge University Press.
Atran, Scott. 2002. *In Gods We Trust: The Evolutionary Landscape of Religion*. Oxford University Press.
Auerbach, Nina. 1995. *Our Vampires, Ourselves*. University of Chicago Press.
Augustine. 1950. *The City of God*. Modern Library.
Barrett, Justin L. 1999. "Theological Correctness: Cognitive Constraint and the Study of Religion." *Method and Theory in the Study of Religion*, vol. 11, no. 4, pp. 325–39.
Barrett, Justin L. 2010. "The Relative Unnaturalness of Atheism: On Why Geertz and Markusson Are Both Right and Wrong." *Religion*, vol. 40, no. 3, pp. 169–72.
Barrett, Justin L. 2011. *Cognitive Science, Religion, and Theology: From Human Minds to Divine Minds*. Templeton Press.
Bartlett, Robert. 2008. *The Natural and the Supernatural in the Middle Ages*. Cambridge University Press.
Beard, Mary, John North, and Simon Price. 1998. *Religions of Rome: Volume 1, A History*. Cambridge University Press.
Bloch, Maurice. 1992. *Prey into Hunter: The Politics of Religious Experience*. Cambridge University Press.
Blum, Jason. 2011. "Pragmatism and Naturalism in Religious Studies." *Method and Theory in the Study of Religion*, vol. 23, no. 2, pp. 83–102.
Boodts, Shari, and Anthony Dupont. 2018. "Augustine of Hippo." *Preaching in the Patristic Era: Sermons, Preachers, and the Audiences in the Latin West*, edited by Anthony Dupont, Shari Boodts, Gert Partoens, and Johan Leemans. Brill, pp. 177–97.
Boyer, Pascal. 1994. *The Naturalness of Religious Ideas: A Cognitive Theory of Religion*. University of California Press.
Boyer, Pascal. 2001. *Religion Explained: The Evolutionary Origins of Religious Thought*. Basic Books.
Boyer, Pascal. 2004. "Out of Africa: Lessons from a By-Product of Evolution." *Religion as Human Capacity: A Festschrift in Honor of E. Thomas Lawson*, edited by Timothy Light and Brian C. Wilson, Brill, pp. 25–43.
Burkert, Walter. 1985. *Greek Religion: Archaic and Classical*. Translated by John Raffan, Blackwell Publishing.

Burkert, Walter. 1996a. *Creation of the Sacred: Tracks of Biology in Early Religions*. Harvard University Press.

Burkert, Walter. 1996b. "Response: Exploring Religion in a Biological Landscape." *Method and Theory in the Study of Religion*, vol. 10, no. 1, pp. 129–32.

Bushnell, Horace. 1910. *Nature and the Supernatural as Together Constituting the One System of God*. Charles Scribner's Sons.

Byrne, Peter. 1988. "Religion and the Religions." *The World's Religions*, edited by Stewart Sutherland and Peter Clarke. Routledge, pp. 3–28.

Cazeneuve, Jean. 1972. *Lucien Lévy-Bruhl*. Translated by Peter Rivière, Harper and Row.

Chaney, Richard Paul. 1978. "Polythematic Expansion: Remarks on Needham's Polythetic Classification." *Current Anthropology*, vol. 19, no. 1, pp. 139–43.

Clark, Stuart. 1997. *Thinking with Demons: The Idea of Witchcraft in Early Modern Europe*. Oxford University Press.

Coleman, Linda, and Paul Kay. 1981. "Prototype Semantics: The English Word Lie." *Language*, vol. 57, pp. 26–44.

Collingwood, Robin G. 1945. *The Idea of Nature*. Clarendon Press.

Cosmides, Leda, John Tooby, and Jerome H. Barkow. 1992. "Introduction: Evolutionary Psychology and Conceptual Integration." *The Adapted Mind: Evolutionary Psychology and the Generation of Culture*, edited by Jerome H. Barkow, Leda Cosmides, and John Tooby. Oxford University Press, pp. 3–15.

Coward, Harold. 1992. "A Hindu Response to Derrida's View of Negative Theology." *Derrida and Negative Theology*, edited by Harold Coward and Jacques Foshay, State University of New York Press, pp. 199–226.

Coward, Harold, and Jacques Foshay. 1992. *Derrida and Negative Theology*. State University of New York Press.

Crombie, I. M. 1962. *An Examination of Plato's Doctrines: Plato on Knowledge and Reality*. Humanities Press.

D'Andrade, Roy. 1995. *The Development of Cognitive Anthropology*. Cambridge University Press.

de Chardin, Pierre Teilhard. 1960. *The Divine Milieu: An Essay on the Interior Life*. Harper.

de Lubac, Henri. 1946. *Surnaturel: études historiques*. Aubier.

de Lubac, Henri. 1967. *The Mystery of the Supernatural*. Translated by Rosemary Sheed, Herder and Herder.

Decock, Lieven, and Igor Douven. 2011. "Similarity after Goodman." *Review of Philosophy and Psychology*, vol. 2, pp. 61–75.

Diels, Hermann. 1960. *Die Fragmente Der Vorsokratiker*. Weidmannsche Verlagsbuchhandlung.

Durkheim, Émile. 1965. *The Elementary Forms of Religious Life*. Translated by Joseph Ward Swain, The Free Press. Originally published 1915.

Durkheim, Émile, and Marcel Mauss. 1963. *Primitive Classification*. Cohen & West Ltd.

Ehnmark, Erland. 1935. *The Idea of God in Homer*. Translated by O. von Feilitzen, Almqvist & Wiksell.

Evans-Pritchard, Edward E. 1937. *Witchcraft, Oracles and Magic among the Azande.* Clarendon Press.
Evans-Pritchard, Edward E. 1965. *Theories of Primitive Religion.* Oxford University Press.
Fitzgerald, Timothy. 1996. "Religion, Philosophy and Family Resemblance." *Religion*, vol. 26, pp. 215–36.
Fitzgerald, Timothy. 1997. "A Critique of 'Religion' as a Cross-Cultural Category." *Method and Theory in the Study of Religion*, vol. 9, pp. 91–110.
Fitzgerald, Timothy. 2000. *The Ideology of Religious Studies.* Oxford University Press.
Geertz, Clifford. 1966. "Religion as a Cultural System." *Anthropological Approaches to the Study of Religion*, edited by Michael Banton, Tavistock, pp. 1–16.
Geertz, Clifford. 1973. *The Interpretation of Cultures.* Basic Books.
Gentner, Dedre, and Mary Jo Rattermann. 1991. *Language and the Career of Similarity.* University of Illinois at Urbana-Champaign.
Gilmore, David D. 2003. *Monsters: Evil Beings, Mythical Beasts, and All Manner of Imaginary Terrors.* University of Pennsylvania Press.
Gnuse, Robert. 1994. "New Directions in Biblical Theology: The Impact of Contemporary Scholarship in the Hebrew Bible." *Journal of the American Academy of Religion*, vol. 62, no. 3, pp. 893–918.
Goodman, Nelson. 1972. "Seven Strictures on Similarity." *Problems and Projects*, Bobbs-Merrill, pp. 437–46.
Green, William Scott. 2006. "What Do We Mean by 'Religion' and 'Western Civilization'?" *Religious Foundations of Western Civilization: Judaism, Christianity, and Islam*, edited by Jacob Neusner, Abingdon Press, pp. 3–23.
Guthrie, Stewart Elliott. 1993. *Faces in the Clouds: A New Theory of Religion.* Oxford University Press.
Guthrie, William K. C. 1967. "Pre-Socratic Philosophy." *The Encyclopedia of Philosophy*, vol. 6, pp. 441–6.
Hallowell, A. Irving. 1955. "The Self and Its Behavioral Environment." *Culture and Experience*, edited by A. Irving Hallowell, University of Pennsylvania Press, pp. 75–110.
Hallowell, A. Irving. 1960. "Ojibwa Ontology, Behavior, and World View." *Culture in History: Essays in Honor of Paul Radin*, edited by Stanley Diamond, Columbia University Press, pp. 19–52.
Harris, Marvin. 1975. *Culture, People, Nature.* 2nd edition, Crowell.
Hirschfeld, Lawrence A., and Susan Gelman, editors. 1994. *Mapping the Mind: Domain Specificity in Cognition and Culture.* Cambridge University Press.
Hocart, Arthur Maurice. 1932a. "Natural and Supernatural." *Man*, vol. 32, pp. 59–61.
Hocart, Arthur Maurice. 1932b. "Letter: Natural and Supernatural." *Man*, vol. 32, pp. 246–57.
Horton, Robin. 1960. "A Definition of Religion, and Its Uses." *Journal of the Royal Anthropological Institute*, vol. 90, pp. 201–26.
Horton, Robin. 1983. "Social Psychologies: African and Western." *Oedipus and Job in West African Religion*, Cambridge University Press, pp. 41–82.
Hudson, W. D. 1977. "What Makes Religious Beliefs Religious?" *Religious Studies*, vol. 13, no. 2, pp. 221–42.
Hultkrantz, Åke. 1979. *The Religions of the American Indians.* Translated by Monica Setterwall, University of California Press.

Hultkrantz, Åke. 1983. "The Concept of the Supernatural in Primal Religion." *History of Religions*, vol. 22, no. 3, pp. 231–53.
Irenaeus of Lyon. 1885. *Against Heresies*. Wm B. Eerdmans Publishing Co.
Jackendoff, Ray. 1983. *Semantics and Cognition*. MIT Press.
Jaeger, Werner. 1947. *The Theology of the Early Greek Philosophers*. Clarendon Press.
Jones, Steve. 1997. "The Set within the Skull." *The New York Review of Books*, November 6, pp. 3–16.
Kaufman, Gordon D. 1960. *Relativism, Knowledge, and Faith*. University of Chicago Press.
Kaufman, Gordon D. 1972. *God the Problem*. Harvard University Press.
Keck, Frédéric. 2008. *Lucien Lévy-Bruhl: Entre philosophie et anthropologie*. Contradiction et participation (Philosophie/Religion/Histoire des idées). CNRS Éditions.
Kenny, John P. 1967. "Supernatural." *New Catholic Encyclopedia*, McGraw Hill, pp. 812–16.
Kenny, John P. 1972. *The Supernatural: Medieval Theological Concepts to Modern*. Alba House.
Klass, Morton. 1995. "The Problem with Supernatural." *Ordered Universes: Approaches to the Anthropology of Religion*, edited by Morton Klass, Westview Press, pp. 25–33.
Koller, John M. 1982. *The Indian Way*. Macmillan.
Lakoff, George. 1987. *Women, Fire, and Dangerous Things: What Categories Reveal about the Mind*. University of Chicago Press.
Le Fanu, Sheridan. 1872. "Carmilla." *In a Glass Darkly*, P. Davies.
Lévy-Bruhl, Lucien. 1931. *Le surnaturel et la nature dans la mentalité primitive*. Alcan.
Lévy-Bruhl, Lucien. 1936. *Primitives and the Supernatural*. Translated by Lilian A. Clare, E. P. Dutton.
Lévy-Bruhl, Lucien. 1975. *The Notebooks on Primitive Mentality*. Translated by Peter Rivière, Harper and Row.
Lévy-Bruhl, Lucien. 1985. *How Natives Think*. Translated by Lilian A. Clare, Princeton University Press.
Lienhardt, Godfrey. 1961. *Divinity and Experience: The Religion of the Dinka*. Oxford University Press.
Linnaeus, Carl. 1735. *Systema Naturae*. Lugduni Batavorum.
Lossky, Vladimir. 2002. *The Mystical Theology of the Eastern Church*. St Vladimir's Seminary Press.
Lovejoy, Arthur O. 1935. "Prolegomena to the History of Primitivism." *A Documentary History of Primitivism and Related Ideas*, edited by Arthur O. Lovejoy and George Boas, John Hopkins Press, pp. 1–22.
Lovejoy, Arthur O. 1936. *The Great Chain of Being: A Study of the History of an Idea*. Harper and Row.
Lyell, Charles. 1851. *Elements of Geology*. Troutman & Hayes.
Martin, Dale B. 2004. *Inventing Superstition: From the Hippocratics to the Christians*. Harvard University Press.
McCauley, Robert N. 2011. *Why Religion Is Natural and Science Is Not*. Oxford University Press.
McLeod, Frederick G. 2000. "Theodore of Mopsuestia Revisited." *Theological Studies*, vol. 61, pp. 447–80.

Medin, Douglas L. 1989. "Concepts and Conceptual Structure." *American Psychologist*, vol. 44, pp. 1469–81.
Mithen, Steven. 1996. *The Prehistory of the Mind: The Cognitive Origins of Art, Religion and Science*. Thames & Hudson.
Mithen, Steven. 1999. "Symbolism and the Supernatural." *The Evolution of Culture: An Interdisciplinary View*, edited by Robin Dunbar, Chris Knight, and Camilla Power, Rutgers University Press, pp. 147–69.
Otto, Walter F. 1979. *The Homeric Gods: The Spiritual Significance of Greek Religion*. Thames & Hudson.
Parmentier, Richard J. 1985. "Semiotic Mediation: Ancestral Genealogy and Final Interpretant." *Semiotic Mediation: Sociocultural and Psychological Perspectives*, edited by Elizabeth Mertz and Richard J. Parmentier, Academic Press, pp. 359–85.
Placher, William C. 1983. *A History of Christian Theology: An Introduction*. Westminster Press.
Pope Pius X. 1907. *Encyclical: Pascendi Dominici Gregis: On the Doctrines of the Modernists*. Angelus Press.
Popper, Karl R. 1962. *Conjectures and Refutations: The Growth of Scientific Knowledge*. Basic Books.
Popper, Karl R. 1972. *Objective Knowledge: An Evolutionary Approach*. Clarendon Press.
Pyysiäinen, Ilkka. 2001. *How Religion Works: Towards a New Cognitive Science of Religion*. E. J. Brill.
Quammen, David. 2003. *Monster of God: The Man-Eating Predator of the Jungles of History and the Mind*. W. W. Norton and Co.
Randall, John Herman. 1970. *Plato: Dramatist of the Life of Reason*. Columbia University Press.
Rappe, Sara. 2000. "Father of the Dogs? Tracking the Cynics in Plato's Euthydemus." *Classical Philology*, vol. 95, no. 3, pp. 282–303.
Reale, Giovanni. 1990. *A History of Ancient Philosophy. II Plato and Aristotle*. Translated by John R. Catan, State University of New York Press.
Rosch, Eleanor. 1978. "Principles of Categorization." *Cognition and Categorization*, edited by Eleanor Rosch and Barbara B. Lloyd, Lawrence Erlbaum Associates, pp. 27–48.
Runciman, W. G. 1969. "The Sociological Explanation of 'Religious' Beliefs." *Archives Européennes de Sociologie*, vol. 10, pp. 149–91.
Saler, Benson. 1994. "Cultural Anthropology and the Definition of Religion." *"The Notion of 'Religion' in Comparative Research," Selected Proceedings of the XVIth Congress of the International Association for the History of Religion, Rome, 1990*, edited by Ugo Bianchi, L'Erma di Bretschneider, pp. 831–36.
Saler, Benson 1997. "Conceptualizing Religion: The Matter of Boundaries." *Vergleichen Und Verstehen in Der Religionswissenschaft*, edited by Hans-Joachim Klimkeit, Harrassowitz Verlag, pp. 27–35.
Saler, Benson. 1999. "Family Resemblance and the Definition of Religion." *Historical Reflections/Réflexions Historiques*, vol. 25, no. 3, pp. 391–404.
Saler, Benson. 2000a. *Conceptualizing Religion: Immanent Anthropologists, Transcendent Natives, and Unbounded Categories*. Berghahn Books.

Saler, Benson. 2000b. "Responses." *Method and Theory in the Study of Religion*, vol. 12, no. 1/2, pp. 323–38.
Saler, Benson. 2004. "Towards a Realistic and Relevant 'Science of Religion.'" *Method and Theory in the Study of Religion*, vol. 16, no. 3, pp. 205–33.
Saler, Benson. 2009. *Understanding Religion: Selected Essays*. Walter de Gruyter.
Sandbach, F. H. 1975. *The Stoics*. W. W. Norton and Co.
Schiller, Friedrich. 1892. *The Gods of Greece, from the German of Schiller: With the Celebrated Suppressed Stanzas Restored*. Grocock and Condliff.
Segal, Robert A. 1989. *Religion and the Social Sciences: Essays on the Confrontation*. Scholars Press.
Selye, Hans. 1950. "Stress and the General Adaptation Syndrome." *British Medical Journal*, vol. 1, no. 4667, p. 1383.
Slone, D. Jason. 2004. *Theological Incorrectness: Why Religious People Believe What They Shouldn't*. Oxford University Press.
Smith, J. Warren. 2002. "'Suffering Impassably': Christ's Passion in Cyril of Alexandria's Soteriology." *Pro Ecclesia*, vol. 11, no. 4, pp. 463–83.
Smith, Jonathan Z. 1998. "Religion, Religions, Religious." *Critical Terms for Religious Studies*, edited by Mark C. Taylor, University of Chicago Press, pp. 269–84.
Smith, Linda B. 1993. "The Concept of Same." *Advances in Child Development and Behavior*, vol. 24, pp. 215–52.
Smith, Wilfred Cantwell. 1962. *The Meaning and End of Religion*. Macmillan.
Sneath, Peter H. A., and Robert A. Sokal. 1973. *Numerical Taxonomy: The Principles and Practices of Numerical Classification*. W. H. Freeman.
Sokal, Robert A., and Peter H. A. Sneath. 1963. *Principles of Numerical Taxonomy*. W. H. Freeman.
Southwold, Martin. 1978. "Buddhism and the Definition of Religion." *Man*, vol. 13, pp. 362–79.
Spiro, Melford E. 1966. "Religion: Problems of Definition and Explanation." *Anthropological Approaches to the Study of Religion*, edited by Michael Banton, Tavistock, pp. 85–126.
Stark, Rodney. 2007. *Discovering God: The Origins of the Great Religions and the Evolution of Belief*. HarperOne.
Stoker, Bram. 1897. *Dracula*. A. Constable & Co.
Stokes, Michael C. 1971. *One and Many in Presocratic Philosophy*. Center for Hellenic Studies; Harvard University Press.
Sullivan, Jack. 1978. *Elegant Nightmares: The English Ghost Story from Le Fanu to Blackwood*. Ohio University Press.
Telfer, William. 1955. *Cyril of Jerusalem and Nemesius of Emesa*. John Knox Press.
Theodore of Mopsuestia. 2011. *De Incarnatione*. Edited by John Behr, Oxford University Press.
Thompson, Stith. 1955. *Motif Index of Folk Literature*. Indiana University Press.
Thompson, Stith. 1964. *The Types of Folktale*. Academia Scientarium Fennica.
Tooby, John, and Leda Cosmides. 1992. "The Psychological Foundations of Culture." *The Adapted Mind: Evolutionary Psychology and the Generation of Culture*, edited by Jerome H. Barkow, Leda Cosmides, and John Tooby. Oxford University Press, pp. 19–136.

Tylor, Edward B. 1958. *Primitive Culture*. Part I: *The Origins of Culture*; Part II: *Religion in Primitive Cultures*. Harper Bros.

Vernant, Jean-Pierre. 1983. *Myth and Thought among the Greeks*. Routledge and Kegan Paul.

Veyne, Paul. 1988. *Did the Greeks Believe in Their Myths: An Essay on the Constitutive Imagination*. Translated by Paula Wissig, University of Chicago Press.

von Wilamowitz-Moellendorff, Ulrich. 1956. *Der Glaube Der Hellenen*. Weidmannsche Buchhandlung.

Wallace, Anthony F. C. 1956a. "Mazeway Resynthesis: A Biocultural Theory of Religious Inspiration." *Transactions of the New York Academy of Sciences*, vol. XVIII, pp. 626–36.

Wallace, Anthony F. C. 1956b. "Revitalization Movements: Some Theoretical Considerations for Their Comparative Study." *American Anthropologist*, vol. LVIII, pp. 264–81.

Wallis, R. T. 1972. *Neoplatonism*. E. J. Brill.

Wiebe, Donald. 1988. "Postulations for Safeguarding Preconceptions: The Case of the Scientific Religionist." *Religion*, vol. 18, pp. 11–19.

Wiebe, Donald. 1990. "Disciplinary Axioms, Boundary Conditions and the Academic Study of Religion: On Pals and Dawson." *Religion*, vol. 20, pp. 17–29.

Wiebe, Donald. 1999. "Appropriating Religion: Understanding Religion as an Object of Science." *Approaching Religion: Part I*, edited by Tore Ahlbäck, The Donner Institute for Research in Religious and Cultural History (Distributed by Almqvist & Wiksell International Stockholm, Sweden), pp. 253–72.

Wittgenstein, Ludwig. 1958. *Philosophical Investigations*. Translated by G. E. M. Anscombe, 3rd edition, Macmillan.

Wolfson, Harry A. 1941. "Hallevi and Maimonides on Design, Chance, and Necessity." *Proceedings of the American Academy for Jewish Research*, vol. 11, pp. 105–63.

Woodbridge, Frederick J. E. 1965. *Aristotle's Vision of Nature*. Columbia University Press.

Wyschograd, Edith. 1981. "The Civilizational Perspective in Comparative Studies of Transcendence." *Transcendence and the Sacred*, edited by Alan M. Olson and Leroy S. Rouner, University of Notre Dame Press, pp. 58–79.

INDEX

analogy. *See also* approximation
   of convenience 31–6
   definition 29
   psychology of similarity with
      approximation 29–31
Anaximander 41, 43–4
Anaximenes 41, 43–4
anthropologists
   on ideation 111
   on "science of religion" 117
   supernatural, use of the term 31
   truth-values of magico-religious claims
      117–18
anthropology, as "the study of culture" or
      "the science of culture" 104
anthropomorphic gods
   gifts of 60
   myths 62–4
   origins 62–6
   power and other attributes 59–60
   rationalizing legends 64–5
   superhuman characters 65–6
apophatic theology 98–9
approximation. *See also* analogy
   definition 29
   psychology of similarity with analogy
      29–31
Aquinas, Thomas 3–4, 56, 70, 91
Ares 60
Aristotle 59
   analogs in philosophy and theology 11
   on God 58
   History of Animals, The 81
   on human mind 50
   Metaphysics 42, 56
   on Milesians 42–3
   Physics 57
   theory of motion 56–7
   theory of nature 56
   theos, use of the term 56, 58
   Unmoved Mover, aka *theos* ("god")
      56–8
Asad, T. 138
   "Anthropological Conceptions of
      Religion: Reflections on Geertz" 137
Athanasius of Alexandria, *On the*
      Incarnation 90
Athena 59–60
Atran, S. 129–30
Auerbach, N. 106–7, 109
Augustine of Hippo 91
   The City of God 80

Boyer, P. 12, 58, 70–1, 102–3, 111–15,
      128–9, 133, 141–2, 146–8
Burkert, W. 58
Bushnell, H. 40
   Nature and the Supernatural as
      Together Constituting the One
      System of God 41
   supernatural, identification of 40

Chaney, R. 145
Christian intellectuals
   on exercise of free will 82
   hierarchy of creation 83
Christian theology
   divine causation, effects of 81
   doctrine of the Trinity 71, 87
   early assertions 91
   prototypical exemplars 140–1
   science and 70
   social relationship between gods and
      humans 97–8

supernatural, use of term 2–3, 56, 92, 96
Word of God, claims of 60–1
Clark, S., *Thinking with Demons: The Idea of Witchcraft in Early Modern Europe* 4
Clement of Alexandria, on Word of God 90
cognitive and evolutionary sciences
　human beings as phenomenal subjects 127–9
　Mithen's approach 131–4
　phylogenetic perspective 129–31
　Religion and culture 126–8
Collingwood, R. G. 42
Cosmides, L. 123
　"The Psychological Foundations of Culture" 121
　Standard Social Science Model 121–6
Cyril of Alexandria 86–8, 92
　on Christ's suffering 87–8
　hupèr phúsin 89
　on supernatural 89

Darwinian theory 130
Democritus of Abdera 45
　atomic theories 46–7
　as the laughing philosopher 45–6
　materialist theology 47
Derrida, J. 98
divinization 90–2
Durkheim, É. 97–8, 123, 126
　on church 98
　The Elementary Forms of the Religious Life 16
　idea of the impossible 20–1, 33–4
　on primitive peoples 18, 21–2
　religion, definition 16–17
　on supernatural 17–20

Eastern Orthodox theologians 69
Ehnmark, E. 60
emanationism
　cosmogonies and cosmologies 94
　experience of union 95–6

Eos 59
Euhemerus 65
　The Sacred Record 64
Euripides 59
Euro-Americans 1, 4–5
　analogy and approximation 29, 31–2
　classical physics 19
　cross-cultural applications 32–3
　divinity's impact on humanity 84–5
　intellectuals 81
　Judeo-Christian god 7–8
　on myth-making concepts 50–1, 64
　nature and natural, ideas on 10, 28
　on negative theology 98
　non-Western societies *versus* 15
　philosophical monism 19–20
　primitive peoples' beliefs 21–2, 24–5
　religion, concept of 27, 140–1
　spatial exteriority, metaphors of 40
　supernatural discourses 1, 4–6, 33
　theistic categories 6
Evans-Pritchard, E. E. 33
　Witchcraft, Oracles and Magic among the Azande 118

Geertz, C. 123, 137–8
genus Homo 132
Goodman, N. 31–2
　seven "strictures" on similarity 29–30
Greeks, ancient
　existence of God 66
　hero cults 92
　literary heritage 38
　literature 91
　metaphysical conceptions 68–9
　Milesian physicists 41–5
　mythology, concept of 64
　paganism 38–9
　rationalizing legends 64–5
　religion and philosophy 58–61
　senses of transcendence 41, 45–6
　supernatual, concepts 38
　Zeus, temple 66
Guthrie, S. 133

Guthrie, W. K. C. 39, 42
    on Milesian philosophers 39, 42

Hallowell, A. I. 33, 45, 52, 130
    on Ojibwa conception of causality 26–8
    "Ojibwa Ontology, Behavior, and World View" 26
    phylogenetic perspectives 25–6
    weasel word expressions 26
Harris, M. 31–2
Hebrew Bible
    conceptions of gods 74
    and creation 74–6
    creator/creature distinction 78–80
    creator, description 76
    Genesis 1 76
    historical truths 75
    idea of an *ex nihilo* creation 76–7
    Israelite monotheism 74
    nature as derivative 77–8
Hecataeus of Teos 65
Hellenism
    origins of the gods 62–3
    religious frames 141
Hephaestus 60
Hesiod 76
    cosmogony 62–3
Hinduism 98
Hocart, M. 31–2
Homer
    Iliad 65
    Odyssey 65
    Tithonus, *story of* 59
Homo sapiens 132–3
Hudson, W. D., on "logical transcendence" 41
Hultkrantz, A. 31–2

Iamblichus 93–4
Irenaeus of Lyon, on Word of God 90

Jaeger, W. 5, 42–3, 78
Jones, S. 93
Judaism 74, 77

prototypical exemplars 140
Justinian, Emperor 86

Kaufman, G. 76
    types of transcendence 41

Le Fanu, S. 101, 110
    Carmilla 105, 107, 109
Leucippus 46
Lévy-Bruhl, L.
    accepting Durkheim's views 23–4, 33
    on affect category of supernatural 24–5
    contrasts with Western views 24
    Le surnaturel et la nature dans la mentalité primitive (*Primitives and the Supernatural*) 23
    Notebooks 23
    primitive mentality 22, 25
Lyell, Sir C., *Elements of Geology* 82

Maimonides 58
Medin, D. L. 136, 145
mind
    modular theory 112–13, 127–8
    monster and 110–15
monsters
    in folklore 114
    and mind 110–15
    phenomenon of "play" 113
    slaying stories 108–10, 112–13

Neanderthals 132–3
negative theology 98–9
    lite and heavy 99
Nemesius of Emesa 82
Neoplatonism
    cosmogonies of Late Antiquity 94–5
    major figures 93
    ontological issues 93–4
neo-Darwinian theory 130
non-Western beliefs 8–9, 29, 31
    religion, concept of 139, 142–3

Odysseus 60

Persaeus 65
Person category, prototypical
    conceptualizations 114–15
Plato 56, 59
    Forms 48
    immortal soul, concepts of 39, 50–6
    Laws, The (Book X) 50
    on myth-making 51
    Orphic and Pythagorean imaginings
        51
    Phaedo 51
    Phaedrus 51–3, 56
    Republic 51–2
    Socratic Method 54
    transcendent forms 48–50
Plotinus 68, 93–7
polysemous 6, 135
polythetic classification 145
Popper, K. R. 127, 136
    Conjectures and Refutations 42
    *Objective Knowledge: An Evolutionary
        Approach* 42
    "observation is called in as a witness"
        43
Porphyry 93, 95–6
Proclus 69, 93
Prodicus of Ceos 65
"*Pülasü*" 103–4

Randall, Jr. J. H. 95
religion
    autonomy of 118–19
    being realistic 135–7
    being relevant 119–22, 126–7
    categories and categorization 143–6
    definitional problem 137–9
    doctrinal 141–3
    evolutionary theory 129–31
    organized 141
    scholarly model 148–9
    scholarly studies, limitations, and
        possibilities 118–22
    science and 69–74, 117
    secularization hypothesis 119
    theism 147

Western conception 139
world 141
Runciman, W. C. 32

Schiller, F.
    "The Gods of Greece" 38
    lamentations 39
science
    Great Chain of Being 81–2
    religion and 69–74
Selye, H., "The General Adaptation
    Syndrome" 134
Sextus Empiricus 47
Smith, J. W. 88
Smith, J. Z. 138
Smith, L. B. 30
Smith, W. C. 137
    Meaning and End of Religion, The 118
social scientists
    supernatural, use of the term 33
    view of supernatural 15–16
Socrates 65, 98
    Socratic Method 54
Spiro, M. E. 9, 139, 147
    religion, definition 61
    on superhuman beings 61–2
Stark, R., supernatural, definition 33–4
Stoker, B. 102, 105
    Dracula 105–10, 114–15
Stokes, M. 42
superhuman
    agents 9, 61–2
    Homeric poems 65–6
supernatural
    agents 9, 146–8
    concept 36
    contrastive sense of natural 11–13
    definition 33
    as hallmark of religion 102–3
    material artifacts 131–4
    mysterious entities 37
    natural/cultural opposition 9–11
    social scientist's view 33–6
    symbolism 131–4
    theological category of 84

Supernatural (American TV series) 3
supra natura, Latin expression 2

Thales 41
Theodore of Mopsuestia 97
    Antioch School of Theology 80
    rational claims 85
    redemptive mission of Christ 83–4
    views on nature 82
theología 68–9
theology
    anthropological implications 72–3
    salient elements 67–8, 70
Theophrastus 42
Theravada Buddhism 146–7
Tooby, J. 123
    Standard Social Science Model 121–6
transcendence, dictionary definition 41

Upper Paleolithic 132

Vampires. *See also* mind; monsters
    British and American vampire novels 106, 109
    in *Carmilla* 105, 107, 109
    in *Dracula* 105–10, 114–15
    family resemblance approach 106
    knowledge of the rules 110
    monster-slaying stories and narratives 108–15
    person category 115
    prototype effects 106–7
    shapes and behaviors 101
Vernant, J-P. 38–9
Veyne, P. 51
    Did the Greeks Believe in Their Myths 63

Wallace, A. F. C. 134–5
    "mazeway resynthesis" 134
Wayuu 103–4
Western Europe
    supernaturals 3–4
    theology, use of the term 69
Wiebe, D. 119, 121
    Åbo Symposium on Methodology in the Study of Religions 120
Wilamowitz-Mollendorff, U. von 58
Wissing, P. 63–4
Wittgenstein, L. 143–5
    on diversity of games 144
Wyschograd, E. 55
    transcendence 40

Zeno the Stoic 65
Zeus 59, 91

www.ingramcontent.com/pod-product-compliance
Lightning Source LLC
Chambersburg PA
CBHW061836300426
44115CB00013B/2408